ANNOYING LOVE
Building Family Faith

James (Jamie) Pettit

Annoying Love

Trilogy Christian Publishers

A Wholly Owned Subsidiary of Trinity Broadcasting Network

2442 Michelle Drive

Tustin, CA 92780

For information, address Trilogy Christian Publishing

Rights Department, 2442 Michelle Drive, Tustin, CA 92780.

For information about special discounts for bulk purchases, please contact Trilogy Christian Publishing.

Manufactured in the United States of America

10 9 8 7 6 5 4 3 2 1

Library of Congress Cataloging-in-Publication Data is available.

ISBN: 978-1-68556-322-6

ISBN: 978-1-68556-323-3

Dedication

Just as it is with most accomplishments in life, we owe so much to so many and in reflection of that opportunity I would like to take a few moments to acknowledge many special people who played a major role in helping to frame my life for this book and giving me the grace to write it. Ultimately, I want to thank my Lord and Savior Jesus Christ for saving a wretch like me and putting my feet on solid ground so I could learn to walk in higher places with God daily!

To my mom and dad (*Dianne & Ray*) who are no longer with us on this side of Heaven, thank you for allowing me to learn so much from your trials and challenges in raising me and my siblings. While you were far from a perfect Godly marriage and often disadvantaged in many unfair facets of your life, you kept us provided for, loved, and encouraged to believe God for better things while allowing us to spread our wings and fly beyond the nest of limited resources.

To my wife... *Kathy* you have definitely been the heartbeat of our family's home as I have truly been the mouthpiece just as we were once prophesied over in that pronouncement many years ago in our family's beginning. I could have never made this journey without you walking by my side in faith and friendship these many years. You are without a doubt a Proverbs 31 woman in so many respects, but to me you are my love and life partner in making our house a home for everyone who came into our life throughout our marriage. I love you deeply and look forward to continuing our Grand Parent journey into better days with more of our blessings to come! This book is dedicated to your faithfulness as a mom and our love as parents together.

To my children... *Christopher, Matthew, Joshua, and Kayla.* As I think about what your lives have meant to me, I am filled with strong emotion and unfathomable love. It's amazing how when seeing you enter this world for the first time in the birthing room that my heart leapt with so much joy and love knowing God had given us such wonderful gifts. You were and still are that to me and your mom. We are so proud of the people of God you are becoming and know without a doubt that great things are in store ahead as you continue this life journey with Jesus as your Lord and Savior. Watching you flourish with your own families gives us hope that God honors faith and his reward is surely worth all the sacrifices we could have ever made for you!

To our Daughters-in-law (love)... *Bri, Arianna, and Kealie.* Your love decision to walk hand and heart with our sons have been a great blessing to Kathy and myself as you have made their lives as well as ours more complete in so many ways. May you continue to serve God and your families as being the heartbeats of faith and friendship for the rest of your lives as believers in Christ holding to the obedience of God's word and walking together in holy matrimony. Without a doubt you have given us some of the sweetest and most beautiful grands any grandparent could ever ask for. We are excited for the next wave of baby boomer blessings coming down the road ahead, and we can't wait to see what God gives us within your fingerprints as fashioned onto their precious hearts as well.

To our only Son-in-law (love)...*Kyle.* You had the toughest assignment in choosing my only baby girl to love and live life together with, but you passed with flying colors to have her hand in marriage. We're honored by your love and respect of our family and our daughter as you continue to walk beside her faithfully as she chases the ministry dreams with you as her faith partner. No hurry, but we look forward to seeing the grandchildren you both will add to the family clan in the next few years. Keep leading her in faith and believing God for greater things !

To my Mother-in-law (love)...*Beadie*. Thanks to you and Joe for raising my wife to be such a Godly and loving woman for me to make this life journey with. You epitomize the role of an awesome mother and I'm glad you allowed me to be a part of your life as well. Thanks for taking my side when needing support and for adding value to our generations as you always do.

To my siblings and extended family...*Ray, Miranda, Preston, Jimmy and Regina*. Thank you for being such a dynamic part of our family's lives as you have honored, supported, and attended so many events and activities over the years that have blessed our family in countless ways. Together we all have shared so many hardships and trials in growing up as children, but thankfully we are seeing the goodness of God being unfolded in our generation as your committed hearts have helped carry the family torch to many others in our Pettit clan as well.

Finally, to so many other family and friends, your love and living life within the sphere of our family influence has added so much value and helped to shape us in ways we will never fully realize. Everyone from pastors and leaders to church family, teachers, neighbors, school mates and besties to our children, have all done so many generous and kind acts toward moving us into a faith modeled experience. Without a doubt, it takes a fully engaged village to develop a family heritage that translates into the next generation, and we are so proud that so many have partnered with our family in such amazing ways to get us to where we are today.

To my friend, Spiritual Father and Apostolic Missionary mentor *Irvin*. Thank you for taking the time to provide a foreword of my first published book, as I greatly value your heart in serving God throughout the decades of tenure in your ministry. You and Linda have been models of faith, consistency, and a true biblical example of what it means to give yourself away for the gospel. Your commitment to the work of the Lord, as well as to the evangelistic ministry of the church and unchurched goes beyond any amount of thanks one could ever offer for your service to God. I have been blessed greatly by you showing me the great window of missions which has opened both my heart and hands go and give in places where the gospel can be planted.

To my Pastor, long- time friend and spiritual advisor, Tony. Thank you for sharing a voice in my first Christian ministry book. I have enjoyed our faith journey together having been one of your sheep, colleagues, pastoral staff, and close friend. You and Tami have been both instrumental influences and key components for helping my spiritual life become better in marriage and family development because of the roles modeled even in the proving grounds of your own challenges. I've always appreciated your counsel as well as the fun times of doing ministry together for over three decades. May God continue to add His grace over you and your family for a wonderful legacy of faith as you have modeled consistently.

For those choosing to read this book. Thank you for taking the time to purchase or obtain this book in some capacity. I have asked the Lord to let this writing be an illuminating light to help you on your spiritual journey into following Jesus Christ and *Building Family Faith*. God bless you and your family as you continue to serve God and build the Kingdom of Heaven at home with all the trappings of what it takes to be a Christian influence within your families both now and in future generations to come!

Foreword

Annoying Love is truly A story of building family faith.

A committed father gives us a play-by-play view of how a family "annoyed each other" into a dynamic relationship with God as central to their family life.

It speaks of obedience that "unlocks the provisions we need from God."

Involvement in each child's life thru play. Watching over their Kingdom growth.

And knowing that this kind of Annoying Love is a "generational conveyance."

A great read for young families wanting to build a nest for eaglets that will one day soar in Christian faith.

Irvin and Linda Rutherford.
Missionary Evangelists, Founders of Global Ministry Teams

Over four decades ago, when Tami and I were engaged to marry, we were very much in love. But we were young, naïve and from vastly different backgrounds. She was from the big city, and I was raised five miles outside of a town of a few hundred. She was raised in a godly family who took her to a wonderful Spirit-filled church every Sunday. My family was one of those families that received a visit every year when the local Baptist church held their Fall Revival services. Praise God, my parents accepted Jesus in their late forties and their commitment made such a difference in our family. During my senior year in college, I accepted Christ because God placed someone who practiced "Annoying Love" in a strategic position in my life.

Early in our marriage, Tami and I heard the statistics about the high divorce rate, and we heard the painful stories of broken families. We knew the odds of a strong, intimate, godly marriage and family were not in our favor. Nevertheless, we believed that somehow our marriage and our family could be different. When we disagreed, which seemed like most of the time, we agreed not to give up on each other and not to quit our marriage. When we fought, which was also quite often, we fought to stay together. We believed that God could help two very different people follow His will, live out His purposes and glorify His name together in their marriage and family. You know what? He did! And I'm so thankful we did our part and God did His part.

Tami and I didn't know it at the time, but we were practicing "Annoying Love." God doesn't want marriages to end in divorce and He doesn't want families to be fragmented. The good news is that it's not supposed to be that way and it doesn't have to be that way. God wants your marriage and family blessed. And He wants you to leave a godly legacy for your children and grandchildren.

That's why I'm so thankful for my close friend, Jamie Pettit's book, *Annoying Love*. Whether you are preparing for marriage, starting a family, or fighting to keep your family together, this book will help you. Jamie writes with raw honesty, giving you Biblical principles and practical ways to strengthen your family and build your faith in God's amazing love.

You won't find easy answers or simplistic solutions for your family relationships. But you will find sincere, time-tested, spiritual guidance that will help you safeguard your family. Then you *too* will be able to establish a godly heritage and leave a legacy that will live on for generations.

Tony L. Cribb
Founding Pastor, Hope Church, South Carolina

Preface

While it may seem odd to have a title like *Annoying Love: Building Faith Families,* there is a reason why I chose to use that as my book text focus. My adolescent children seemed to like the usage of this metaphor to describe our responses when it came to something my wife and I said regarding a permission issue or would not allow them to do with friends while they were living at home. To them we seemed to rain on some of their parades of activity too often and it just didn't sit well for their insatiable appetites for teenage fun. Granted we were (are) far from perfect parents but for us as their leaders in trying to maintain our faith household, we made hard calls that obviously rubbed them the wrong way because it wasn't what they wanted necessarily but what we felt they needed to be constrained by. This cry of "you're annoying" became a badge of courage and commitment for us since as their parents we desired to keep the slack out of line of permissiveness when it came to things that seemed borderline or sketchy to us. Of course they made it through those days and moved on as adults mostly unscathed from our "over-bearing" behavior to enjoy full and fun lives now in adulthood. Yet in the process, they had takeaways for building homes of faith for their own families. As of now it's been working out for their ultimate good, as we did leave many God deposits along the journey with our annoying family brand of love as well!

So, in sensing the leading of the Lord to finally venture more into writing and in particular this book (*Annoying Love*), I likened this title to how God has approached us through Jesus Christ. You see the Bible says that God was reconciling man to himself through Christ, and still does today thankfully. Despite the fact that men and women in scripture have historically rejected and reviled God, He was always and will ever continue to reach out His great love through the elements of faith by grace. And while mankind continues even in this modern age to push back against this annoying love through the sacrifice of Jesus Christ, the Father's heart still waits by the front porch for more prodigals to find their way back home to his embrace. God won't quit on anyone and even some of the patriarchs such as Moses, Jonah, and Peter got annoyed at God for His persistent love because it didn't give up on reconciling mankind to Himself. I'm glad for God's annoying love because He came after me as a young adolescent, and while I made a right choice to follow Him in that moment, my walk at times into early adulthood had incurred many stumbling blocks along the way. Oh, but God is good all the time! If you're reading this, I'm sure you can testify as well of the goodness and the faithfulness of our Lord Jesus Christ. So go ahead and give Him a praise right now. Make it loud and be proud!

The premise of this book is written to encourage those in parenting or leadership roles within the home to hang in and hold on with building the faith foundations you are trying to develop in your homelife. Today's informational world is so much more complex and difficult to navigate with all the social media influences and cultural anomalies weighing heavily in the mix of decision making for family life. My trust is that you will be inspired less by my words but more by our God to keep the baton close in hand and run your race with boldness and resolve. We need to take back the ground that has been yielded to unseen enemies in the past few generations where we see our children starting to pay the price for our lack of fortitude when it comes to leading forward with faith. Moms, dads, aunts, uncles, sisters, brothers, families, and even friends, you have what it takes in

Jesus Christ to express an Annoying Love every day and help mold minds and hearts for the Kingdom of Heaven. Don't give slack to this proverbial mantra of annoying love for it will accomplish what you purpose for it to do if you just do it!

TABLE OF CONTENTS

Chapter One – How It All Started

Have you ever been in situations where some thing or somebody just kept pursuing you over an issue and it just got under your skin to the point it felt like they were becoming a nuisance? I am sure the answer is an emphatic YES, so don't feel alone. For me, I think about a little cartoon as a kid where this little dog who was feisty and mouthy would jump around back and forth in the face of this much bigger and stronger bulldog. He was constantly talking and asking about what they could do next or what did he want him to do for the bigger dog. Finally the irritated bigger bulldog stopped in his gate and swatted his paw at the runt dog knocking him across the yard, while saying "Ah, shut up!" To that the little feisty dog would peel himself up off the ground and just be on his merry way again. For the runt dog he was incredibly persistent in trying to play up to his much-adored hero but for the bigger dog he only saw the antics as annoying and just a pesky kissing up motif rather than a real admiring youngster.

So, what about you? What things are events do you remember where someone went the extra mile to keep pressing you to remember something they needed you to do? Maybe it was simply a kind act on their part to make sure you stayed on task to follow a schedule as to your commitments. Today, there are individual specialist given just such jobs to make sure that their leader or boss stays on track and keeps meeting the requirements from day to day. We call them personal assistants and their roles are to be the bad guy many times as to keeping one's agendas fulfilled while making sure that certain demands and appointments are adhered to ongoing. In many cases while their boss expects them to perform their duties admirably and successfully, the hard truth is that the boss often grows weary of this constant push and will ultimately find it annoying as well. We all like the subtle reminders of little things to help us keep moving forward in our day but often we do take exception many times to things that qualify as annoying even if they meet a requirement for keeping us on track when necessary.

In fact, part of the inspiration for writing this book was conceived out of a constant blurb of "You're Annoying," muddled exasperatingly on numerous occasions by one or more of our children. There were too many times to count simply because our children resented our parental persistence in providing strong emphasis and consistency in matters. Yet we believed they were not as passionate about it to address, nor entirely conclusive about when it came to meeting certain necessary objectives. In fact, this kind of ongoing sentiment morphed into a thing of humor at times as we began in unison as "The Parents" who took a sort of ego pride in helping them quote it back to us. At their declaration of annoying we began to remind them that it was our job to be annoying as parents, and that at some point they too would be likewise in the same future position as parents as well. Thankfully, that day has come for half of our grown children with the younger half still in waiting for their moments to step into parenthood. So to the point of this love annoyance that has become and will continue to be a vital part of our lives ongoing. Truly at some juncture in life everyone will serve to be someone else's "Annoying" good or bad.

It's not like parents or just everyday people start out to become annoying to others but somehow over time and with continued consistency that mantra begins to envelope itself through the course of activity and takes on its own nature. For the ones who know this, a major part of our love duty is to keep emphasizing and supporting the hallmarks of faith and family as well as dozens of other endeavors. This determined effort will help raise God-fearing and well-balanced children who will one day reflect the right values that make for the right kind of posterity. You must as an individual or as a parent become intentional in both demonstrating and developing others in order for it to finally plant in their heart enough to grow crops of blessing. Proverbs describes it like this, train up a child in the right way to go and in time when they are older, they will come back to it and find the pathway. I'm sure there are many parents thinking *yeah right! I tried it but my kids are the exception and seem to be lost for good.* To that I would say, just hold on and don't let go of your hope or faith for God is able to do greater things above our own thoughts and ideas. Their stories are not yet over, and God is still writing their chapters with so many decisions and discoveries that can prove to lead them back home. Our part, as leaders, is to continue to be that annoying love model so we don't grow weary enough to faint and lose heart. Even if we haven't done all the right things the Bible teaches that in mentoring and parenting God is still able to bring fruit from just a few good seeds we scattered in their heart along the way. Jesus gave a great parable on seed sowing with the results reflecting the fact that in every place good seed falls even if it is good or bad soil there is potential for growth. I choose to believe God for the good seed to land in productive soil and bring about a great return, and I pray for crop failure for any bad seed that perhaps was sown wrongly or incorrectly so as to not bring about any harvest.

As you can understand life is a marathon, so we don't get ahead by sprinting out front with some new idea or philosophy. Steady plodding brings about a prosperous harvest, but hasty speculation will often lead to spiritual bankruptcy if we are just in it from a get quick results standpoint. No, annoying love is always necessary in the life of a believer in so many facets and we will be looking to exploit that kind of opportunity as we move forward in this book. In fact, one of the most popular definitions of annoying is something that is bothersome and irritating or can cause one to feel exasperated or impatient. Now you are probably thinking that an annoying love is not a good thing then, but I would challenge that thought to say that the context for its meaning is everything. Love in and of itself has many avenues of reflection that all play key roles in not only developing a heart of a person but also a life of passion as well. The fact that men and women from different opinions or persuasions can collectively embrace one another in matrimony and substantiate a lifelong relationship is proof enough that annoyances can be positive if rooted in right love. How else can they learn to accept their differences except they continue to adjust on the fly giving grace and concessions to the very things that make them individuals yet binds their hearts as one? Proverbs concludes that just as iron sharpens iron, so one person will always sharpen another. You can only get a sharp blade to cut precise for so long and then it will dull itself over time. The metal sharpening tool acts in many ways as an annoyance gage generating a counterculture measure toward the metal blade thus rendering itself as a resistance to cut away the dull edge while leaving behind the sharpened blade in its wake. A process absolutely necessary for making the tool cut more productive each time!

If you think about it from a deep-sea perspective in nature, an oyster does not create its greatest masterpiece within its shell without it first incurring an irritant inside the lining of its shell wall. As a result of secreting the internal solution to protect itself from harm's way, then ultimately it results in creating a beautiful pearl as a secondary effect of addressing the annoyance. Seems reasonable to believe that it will also work in real life for virtually anyone who takes the time and applies the energy to see it through. Pearls are considered valuable commodities to be bartered with and rarely ever lose their valuation in any economy. In fact, I recently watched a video of how certain Caribbean oyster farmers create the pearls faster by instigating the lowly crustacean to ingest the pseudo irritant capsule and trigger the oyster to begin its handy work. By helping them to stir up their response to secreting their solution it literally grew the pearl at a much faster clip than the natural way they have done for millennia.

Point being, there are things in our lives that though they might be irritating or aggravating, each one can and will play great roles in helping to shape our lives in the framework that we may not want necessarily, but we definitely need in order to complete the work God is trying to do in our lives. No one would ever desire to create pain in their life just for kicks and giggles in order to garner lessons learned in some life situations, yet because it happens, we are made better for the journey than just having learned easy lessons without it. Babies are wonderful gifts from God to parents but unless a mother endures the pain of childbirth whether natural or cesarean, she will never realize the joy of holding her own precious infant and reaping the rewards of her married life with the child's father. So in circling back to where this "Annoying Love" dubbing began, that we have received from our children, we have real life takeaways. While my wife and I never intended to become annoying in our parenting endeavors or even exasperating toward what our children perceived as such, we are glad that we did and still do to some degree employee this persona. This important characteristic has been our guiding post for helping our children tow-the-line along through those challenging adolescent years as we have successfully launched them into adulthood with strong foundations to build on. We are now beginning to see them produce longstanding fruitfulness in their own lives for their marriages and its overflowing into our wonderful grandchildren as well.

One can always argue with the methods utilized when it comes to parenting but we all have to live in the revelation of how we discern the Spirit of God leading us to implement biblical techniques within the scope of our human capacities. We absolutely have to walk in our own understanding by faith and carry the torch to light the path for what we desire to substantiate within our families. There will always be others along the way to help shape these decisions either by adding value to the model mix, or by simply offering encouragement good and bad to some degree that will support this journey. There is no included set of directions for parenting like you find when you purchase a product that requires "some assembly" which will allow success to complete it 99% of the time if you follow it through completely. Yeah, I know some of those decisions can be confusing and hard to manage but parenting or just merely dealing with life issues can be so different that no one else can solve your dilemmas when they happen yet there is help available. This is exactly why God gave us his ultimate plan through understanding His scriptures and having fellowship with the Holy Spirit to help shape our parenting pathway. He gives us enough human latitude to walk it forward in faith one day at a time. We made it and so will you! It just takes time and being consistent as much as you can while trusting, hoping, and praying that the God of mercy will make His grace abound at all times so you can receive the sufficiency to achieve those things you have believed for in life.

God is good all the time, and all the time God is good, so take courage in knowing He desires for you to prosper in all things even as your soul desires to. Remember there will always be your part to go along with God's part but He makes it a unique partnership, so it works for our good even if we fail at times. That is definitely good news to all of us who keep getting back up after failing forward. Proverbs declares that the righteous or good intentioned person may fall seven times in his pursuits, but he continues to rise after each occasion because there is strength in knowing he has God to bolster him in each failing. You my friend have that same success capacity as it doesn't take a Marvel Superhero to parent, but it does take us marveling at a God who will supply all of our needs according to his unlimited resources in Christ Jesus. He always provides an exhaustless measure of grace in all sufficiency for every good work such as parenting so we can understand that it is his good pleasure for us is to prosper in every way when it comes to our leadership roles. Parenting is not a chore per se, but it has a strong posture of serving at the highest level because it requires one to self-examine a heart that is selfish in enjoying an unhindered adult life. At the same time, it creates a dynamic that promotes a selfless act of submission to someone else's needs. Jesus said it best that the greatest measure of any position in the Kingdom of Heaven could be found in serving one another as an ongoing lifestyle commitment. Sounds like the King of kings knows full well what He is talking about having continually demonstrated that approach during His ministry time on earth. It's amazing how this transition begins the very moment that newborn baby gets handed to mom and dad in the hospital. Little do they know at that significant moment that they have received one of the greatest gifts their hearts will ever embrace. A baby changes everything and a parent begins a journey of faith, hope and love, but the greatest is still love. Not just any love, but rather an annoying love in God. How God must marvel at His creation's ability and willingness to partner with Him to bring forth gifts found in the treasure chest of an infant's heart. How then should we not consider our roles as of the utmost importance knowing full well, we have these blessings to shape in life learning.

Chapter Two – What It Means for You!

So, if you have established this mantra of Annoying Love or you are still in pursuit of achieving this at some juncture, I want to first breakdown this concept not only as to what it means for you, but what it is not at the same time. Stephen Covey had a principle in one of his best-selling books that suggested one to begin with the end in mind as you develop highly effective skills for life and business. It may seem difficult in its scope, but the reality of it is so simple that most people skip right past it because we think there is something better out there that we might miss and if we are not careful. Many, unfortunately, will simply gloss over what is ultimately staring them in the face. The truth is most people would not just jump into a car and take off on a vacation trip and then decide later what direction to take not sure where they want to end up driving but instead winging it to see what happens. I understand that in this modern age that there are those who might would do this sort of spontaneous thing, but reasonably logical people (with children) would try to at least to map out a strategy. The planners would book a few hotel rooms, or at least have a game plan for what they want to do with how their budgeting needs would work so as to not create a journey of frustration and angst. Likewise, those who have pledged to live their life in such a way as to promote the gospel faith desire to bring along a family with them to enjoy and employ this Christ centered lifestyle. It does require a defined strategy which is an important element of planning your future destination for a strong spiritual lifestyle and purposed goal development.

Before we move forward, it is important to understand that the annoying love way of life should never be about creating a divergent heart or attitude that seeks to promote a weird philosophy whereby others view your lifestyle as opposing biblical standards. In fact, it should not posture your life to become or display a self-absorbed faith in terms of how you are living outrageously different in that you are out there so far that you lose sight of the goal. The life of love in any God-fearing setting is always tethered to a constraint of standards as demonstrated by the ministry of Jesus while He was here on earth. In other words, when you achieve the "dubbing" of being annoying in your life by your children or even others, it should reflect how God handles us with His love. There is ample grace but there are also restraints and rewards which are concluded within the scope of how you live and serve others. The Bible teaches that children are a gift from the Lord and he who has them has received a great blessing and reward from the Father in Heaven. When we view them as such, we then take on a position of serving and equipping them to become prize gifts back to God so they will one day take on that very same nature. The cool thing is as this is happening within their immature minds, some will view it as suppression or annoyance. As they translate from child to adolescent to adult this unique bridge into their mind begins to stir their hearts with a transformative power that only God can provide through His Spirit. Thus, they become understanding of what your annoying love has done for them even though it has given them moments of disdain and irritation. It has also provided for them great insight into unconditional love, forgiveness, and hope filled living as well as building a legacy of faith. These qualities will move them forward to demonstrate the same love posture one day, albeit in their own mind and heart perspective.

In elementary terms, annoying love describes a strong commitment to faith, family, and future. If you go back say at least twenty-five years ago or more, these were foundational truths and elements of traditional lifestyles that did not require great efforts of focus because they had become embedded in the very fabric of our modern society. Because of the influence of the Christian church, which was experiencing growth, these values were being permeated into many parts of our cultural communities after decades of multiple war and economic impacts. Those years had left America reeling from their blights. Families had a longing to be settled in with a desire for peace and safety through strong moral values among other things which followed those turbulent time in the Forties, Fifties, and Sixties. Even the Seventies and Eighties were emerging as cultural anomalies for pushing these defined boundaries in various facets. Yet, there was still a grass roots establishment of Christian beliefs that help to fuel conservative values and minimize the takeover of society. After the turn of the twenty-first century, our current new millennia trends of conservative and biblical values have been beaten back severely. A new exposure to a greater scope of social media and non-traditional lifestyles have now become the influence of our modern society. Acceptance to non-biblical lifestyles and values have steadily been pushing back the Christian Church influence which seems to have lost its focus as a strong force for shaping and refining our modern-day contemporary culture.

I could write more here on this topic, but for this book I want to keep on point and that being about love. Love that is constant in its focus, consistent in its endeavors, and connecting in its generations is what the gospel of our faith is really all about. A half a century ago, this type of love was not annoying but expected, respected, and protected by the very framework of our traditional society. Today, it has to be planned and purposed with intentionality otherwise it will not pass from one generation to the next with the necessary fervor needed to combat an ever-changing society. What does this mean for me one might ask? It means everything, obviously. I am amazed as I recall my adolescent challenges and then reflect upon how different they were for my own children, and this is only one generation removed, yet so much change has taken place. Passing notes, talking, and chewing gum would garner a swift but effective paddling in my years from middle to high school. Twenty-five years later in my children's school, getting in trouble was now a result of social media and (or) cell phone usage. Instead of correcting the problem students were made to sit in a detention hall for an hour which ultimately proved worthless as far as punishment went. Of course, now we see almost everything taking place in adolescent society, so it is up to us to turn the tide and rescue our children with Christian values again and this requires raising the spiritual flagpole higher.

Admittingly, it is an uphill battle because so much has changed and though biblical beliefs. These were once prominent buffers in society, they have now been characterized as Anti-American or Anti-Cultural because they defined boundaries that oppose other's lifestyles. While we can't make people live a certain way outside our immediate influence, we can elicit a behavior as both parents and leaders to help shape the narrative of those we have influence with ongoing. This annoying love mantra has to be front and center of your faith because your future depends on it as does our society. No amount of legislature can fix what ails us, but the power of God can and will work through our efforts to will and work for His good pleasure. The term each one can reach one is important because this faith philosophy becomes accumulative as it moves down the legacy tree of life. The Bible states that one will put a thousand to flight, but two will put ten thousand to flight in the same regard which for the believer is an exponential hope for posterity. Your ultimate takeaway from your faith life with a love that keeps giving and growing will transcend all the exterior influences that only create a facade of acceptance because real love covers a multitude of wrongs. Those propping up an artificial way of living without a God type of love will in the end find their houses toppled over by the storms that continue to come and rage in the sands of unsustainable foundations. Make sure that the places you are choosing to build your family values on have been erected with wisdom. They will define Godly character as stalwarts to anchor your house whenever challenges come along as they will come in time, but you have a hope because of Jesus Christ. As the old gospel hymn so aptly put it, *My hope is built on nothing less than Jesus's blood and righteousness. I dare not trust the sweetest frame, but wholly lean on Jesus's Name. On Christ the solid Rock I stand. All other ground is sinking sand. All other ground is sinking sand*. Are you anchored to His firm foundation as well?

How you live and who you choose to love in Christ is just as important as anything else you could ever do in your time as a believer as well as a parent or guardian of children. If they are born of your flesh or whether you have chosen to parent them through some other adoptive means does not discount your role in helping create the opportunity to build a household of faith. Regardless of the positioning for your immediate oversight, we are commanded to love and to give our life in learning to serve others while leaning into the strength of the Holy Spirit. The more we pursue God's way of becoming less of yourself and begin increasing our spirituality in more of his nature. We will find that this way of living allows for that annoying love to grow unhindered in our hearts while producing the necessary fruitfulness. That will generate an ultimate harvest of blessing that we desire to see take place in time. Moving the needle to a true north compass setting will require an enormous effort not only with our children and home life but also within the context of our marriage and personal devotion to God on a daily basis. The exciting part is we get that privilege to serve beyond our own self.

Chapter Three – Understanding the Way of Love

John 3:16 is one of the most noted Bible passages in the New Testament and rightly so because it demonstrates not only the character of who God is, but also what He is in the context of His nature and desires. When you really think about what that verse implies, you will begin to get the overwhelming understanding of how grand and great the love of God really is. At least there is an inkling of what that reality has become in faith. What parent in their right mind would willingly yield their ONLY sinless child who was such a saint to humanity as a sacrificial pardon for mankind? This was done while knowing that a sinful creation in no way, shape, or form even deserved to have any exemption in any form. The answer, strikingly, is simple. Plan A for this world has always been that Christ would die once for all of us because God in His sovereignty and omnipotence had begun with the end in mind. He (God) who knows no bounds of time or space had decided before the foundations of the world that a Spotless Lamb would have to be sacrificed in order to redeem a lost society that could never deliver itself. In fact the story of Abram becoming Abraham through offering his son as the sacrifice was the precursor for Jesus becoming that atonement once and for all. God was only testing to see if Abram would be willing to yield his long-awaited child of promise as a measure to understand if mankind had the capacity to be all in for God as the redemption of the world. Isaac was never going to be the spotless lamb God required for sacrifice, but Abram did prove that through his obedience and willingness to yield his only son that he would become Abraham. He became the father of nations by trusting fully in Yahweh that there would be a future and a hope for his life ahead. Obedience provides the key to unlock provisions we need from God and this patriarch demonstrated just how to open doors from God for successful faith living.

Talk about a legacy of dynamic proportions! The Father of our Faith Abraham, held in his heart the balance for the future of all generations to experience the grace and mercy of such a loving and kind God. Scripture says in Hebrews chapter eleven that because of his demonstration of faith in giving up Isaac freely it was reckoned to him as being righteous. In other words, it was not that Abraham in any measure possessed this right standing with God but because of the yielded trust expressed before the almighty. He was made as righteous thus allowing God to insert Christ into the picture millennia later and seal the salvation deal for all mankind. Just think, our opportunity to occupy a place in the Kingdom of Heaven today was perpetrated as a result of someone else's obedience toward their child in a parallel posture. That got the attention of God. This helped promote redemption by this blessing thousands of years later at the cross and still goes on even into eternity. If that is not an annoying love, I don't know what is! God would not give up on His creation. He thought to terminate mankind at the great flood because of the evil that had spread but spared Noah and his family. He thought to terminate the Israelites in the desert for their hard-heartedness but because of Moses's pleas, He relented. And yet, with Abraham, He finally found a willing human heart to obey Him. Granted, Abraham was not without his share of shortcomings and flaws which likely led to some of the delays he experienced before becoming a century old Father. Either way. Destiny was fulfilled, promises were kept, and redemption was again assured for all eternity. What a loving Father our God is, was and will always be. John, the Apostle who is accounted for as penning the famous salvation passage stated emphatically that

God loved His creation so much that He gave his one and only son Jesus. This declares that whoever might choose to believe in Him would not die lost but would have an eternal state of life with Christ. Surely, he had fully grasped the historic significance of his Rabbi and Mentor Jesus Christ. Most definitely John understood this more from his discipled way of life than any other opportunity could hold. It pays to follow Christ as a disciple daily!

As I watched this passage play out in the TV production series called *The Chosen* currently being played in a video TV series, it was neat to see how the writers and directors portrayed. The show stays very closely with the writings of the New Testament scriptures and brings scriptures to life. In fact the video series gave such a vivid portrayal of Nicodemus as he struggled to understand the words of Christ that though they resonated in his heart, his carnal mind could not break away from his religious allegiance to what he knew in his life a Pharisaic Rabbi. In the end, we have to hope that as time went forward perhaps Nicodemus found his way back to the cross where his salvation could be found in the Messiah he passed on when his time came to choose his path to the cross. So many people today miss on the redemption elements of what Jesus did for all mankind. We are such a sinful world today with so many things abounding in every direction to render us as anti-Christ in our culture. Of course, every generation has faced this storyline throughout millennia as evil begets itself if not for the repentance and return of people to God in revival or renewal. Today's believers are not much different from those in generations past who were looking for a deliverer to save them out of the evil and tyranny when oppression began to close in around Christians for one reason or another. The early church had such an expectation that the Messiah who had finally come would take his throne and overthrow the Roman rulers. The reality is God does not come to take sides, he takes over and promotes His redemption agenda only!

You see, when God comes, He comes to transform and translate a Kingdom mindset into the very fiber of His creation. Why else would God call a young virgin woman such as Mary and impregnate her with His Holy Spirit as to create a human child to be born and yet have the divinity as part of His pedigree? God has never wanted it to be us and Him. He always wanted His most prized creation to become in Him, and He in us. That is why He put God incarnate inside of a mother to carry the presence of God and through child birthing yield a sacrificial savior to redeem us back to Himself. Surely God was in Christ reconciling mankind back to Himself and as the scripture so distinctly settles it. He [Jesus] who never participated in willful sin became that very outcome [death] of sin that we might become positioned for right standing with God in Christ Jesus. An annoying love is a love of exchange. It's a love that keeps prevailing and moving throughout epochs of time to substantiate what needs to take place in order for the right things to happen as they are destined to be. There have always been prophecies given directly by God through Holy men and women of renown historical positions to declare the coming of the Messiah. Yet, without the elements of faith and men like Abraham giving of themselves for the cause of Christendom, those words may have fallen short of their measure. We know that the promises of God have never failed in achievement because He is not a man that He should lie, and His word is exalted above His name. In other words, if someone receives a calling but fails to meet or achieve obedience in God's plan, He simply raises up another person in that same place to fulfill His will and work.

A case in point is found in the old testament story of King Saul which you can read about in the first book of Samuel starting around chapter nine and continuing forward into where it begins to crossover into King David's life. When you come upon Saul's mention and begin to read his storyline you discover that he was not overly impressive in any facet and very likely an introvert to some degree. His most noticeable quality at that time seemed to be that he was humble in his self-reflection. He had a simple ancestry lineage of which he did not think that highly of, that he was a man of a tall stature head, and shoulders above his peers which gave rise to his kingly choosing. The truth is, he was not on anyone's list of qualified candidates to become a leader let alone to become Israel's first king. The crazy thing is that the people of Israel only wanted a king because all the other nations had one and they were so unfaithful when it came to following God through the guidance of Judges or Elders who ruled them. Because their hearts had turned to wanting a king to rule over them God was obliged because of his love covenant to give them their choice which turned out to be Saul. In his early days, Saul seemed to have the heart to serve God in his role as king, but it did not take long for his ego to get the best of him. Unfortunately, he lost sight of who he was and who had given him that royal opportunity and it only took a short time for him to begin heading down a path that would create a divergent heart toward God. We find him being responsible at first glance helping to support his father by looking for runaway donkeys and later being caught up with the prophets to the degree that he was associated as being among them. Great traits to have accomplished, but without a heart for God things went south in a hurry. Because of his pride and arrogance he transgressed into things that were forbidden for him to do as God's leader. Saul failed to fulfill full-on obedience to his spiritual calling and because of those wrong choices, the prophet Samuel let him know that he had been rejected by God to continue his family's lineage as Kings over Israel.

David enters the story after being anointed by Samuel the prophet to be the future replacement king and defeats Goliath because he was a true man of faith and character. While he helped to deliver the nation of Israel from the Philistine Armies, he spent many years running and hiding as a hunted man until Saul's tragic death allowed him to assume his appointed role as King of Israel. In the end, God sought to find a man after His own heart in order to lead Israel forward in a faith to choose him and obey His commandments. The takeaway here is significant for believers in that God was again working to reconcile his people to himself despite their defiance against him. He could have let Saul's heritage continue on and allowed harm to befall the nation of Israel, but God had a better plan through his appointment of David as King. This serves as an example for us to understand how choosing an obedient path can be such a powerful tool is to employ God's blessings over everything we have and do for promoting our family faith. There is no other acceptable way!

We all can be so much like Saul in our own way as well. While we may not think of ourselves as being defiant in such a hostile way as he was, the truth is any hesitation or lack of obedience on our part is simply just as wrongly motivated. We see that displayed for us as parents in children who learn skills of manipulation and defiance even before they become school aged. It is our mandated role to help remove that iniquity out of their life through love and discipline so that their will is broken firmly, but their spirits are completely preserved. Always easier said than done since each child has their own temperament to deal with as some are easy to maneuver forward. Other children can become really challenging and vexing to degrees that really can cause concern both in present and future opportunities. How we handle these things are what gives us that ability to love, forgive, and encourage our families through the demonstration of daily living in the admonition of Christ. When it seems so hard to do within our own abilities we have to cling to the Bible for wisdom. The good news is that we have the grace of God and presence of His Holy Spirit there with us at all times buffering and sharpening us through wisdom via the word of God. The fact is for most parents this event is a trial-and-error process guaranteed to cause heartburn and heartache during the learning curve. Yes, your children will be impacted as you mature in your defined parenting roles, but the cool thing is that you grow together, and they have a real sense that you are always for them no matter what. This is where annoying love begins its best work in both you and your children. As I mentioned previously about iron as sharpening each other. Your life as a parent is also being shaped by God and family because just as our kids have to have rough edges taken off of them as they grow, you will also have to have some jagged corners rounded off as their parents as well. Again, we don't come as fully assembled parents in knowing how to handle from babies to adults, so it is an on-the-job training process for many on a daily basis. We can't grow weary in doing well because we will reap the rewards in days ahead if we don't give up too soon. You can do this! God never gives us things we cannot handle without first giving us the resources inside of us to make it happen. Sometimes, you have to dig deep to pull out the tools but just know that with God, you can do all things through Christ who gives you the strength every day.

Throughout the ages of time, God has demonstrated what it means to love, forgive, and bring His people into the promises He has destined for their lives. Many have rejected and paid the ultimate price of not entering into the blessings that were purchased for them, and the spiritual rest that is available through Jesus Christ. The heritage you leave behind as you move forward in living your faith needs to be about building Kingdom. I once heard it said that it's not what you leave behind that will matter when you are gone, but what you send ahead while you are still on earth. While there is truth to that saying, I believe the reality is you can do both if you just purpose it for yourself and be intentional. Proverbs reveal that a good man leaves an inheritance of wealth and blessings to his children's children. The transfer of a legacy implication is not specifically just about money, but rather inclusive of prosperity of the soul, mind, and spirit as well. What better way to impact your family as a parent than to create this lifestyle as you are building your world around you with those who are special in your life. The way of love is hard to fathom for those on the outside of the spiritual scope. In fact, scripture reminds us that the things of a spiritual nature cannot be understood by the carnal minded since they are discerned by the Holy Spirit residing inside of a believer, but they can be caught if pursued in God.

However, what does resonate to the world is displays of love actions done out of a heart of submission within the gospel influence. People tend to stand up and take notice when there has been a reference point of activity by someone that shows an unselfish way of love given without any regard for what's in it for them. We see this often during times of great catastrophes where groups rally behind communities for support and offer unlimited resources for help. As parents and leaders you will need this same heartbeat to approach your home with a fierceness of commitment to hold the line. When this happens on a consistent basis then the true way of love has been exemplified and the context of an annoying love will become more magnified to others as a result. Achieving an acceptable standard in spiritual expectations within your home will become a reality as you build this framework within a strategic faith-based environment. Both you and your family will have an anchor of attachment to initiate the foundational constructs of where you want to place your spiritual homelife once this lifestyle commitment takes place within your heart.

Chapter Four – Make It Real but Keep It Fun

Now that we have taken a look at some pieces of what an annoying love is and what it can become, it's time to assess what it can do for you as you begin to apply some of the tenants of this faith filled lifestyle. I think it is only fair to give some parameters and boundaries as to how this mantra can be developed by you within your family structure. How you maneuver it throughout your life to become hallmarks of foundational truth will build long lasting friendships as well. As I think back regarding my childhood and even into adolescent years, I can remember myself growing from being a timid youngster into a very self-assertive and socially engaging individual which has helped me to morph into this more mature person I have become today. Some of that childhood shaping was not all good influences that made me accelerate and achieve because the given models were so good that all I had to do was follow a pattern and it would get me there. No, in fact many if not most of these external influences were very challenging and even hurtful growth pains that forced me to evaluate who I was and how I was going to posture myself as a result of those impacts. I had come from a humble means where my parents were not affluent in any regard and neither of them had ever formerly finished with a high school graduation diploma. They were a hard-working and self-reliant couple who were scratching out a family path for me and my three siblings to learn and grow from their shortfalls in life. While we had to settle for lesser things in terms of buying power, nonetheless all siblings learned many valuable tools in how not to conduct financial decisions. Because of those challenges that came with our parent's lack of not applying good stewardship with resources, we developed a desire to prove that there was a better path forward if we do the life events with more wisdom.

None of us would trade those childhood life lessons today for the internal drive that developed our fuel for successes along this journey for becoming better in many life applications. We are all very thankful that our parents had the recognition to encourage us to be better than they were when it came to handling resources. Their sacrifices were many. Some not necessary because of bad decisions but many came to be because life happens, and you have to adjust on the fly if you want to take care of your family. Our mom and dad did that daily, so we were better because their annoying love kept moving us forward in faith. Albeit, to us kids in those days it had major waves of frustration in making our provision happen. Yet, it created a stark promotion for our achievements in reaching heights that they were never able to achieve in their lives. Looking back now, it seems surreal that those things that were so bothersome to our way of thinking and made life uncomfortable many times in those moments were also the very trials or challenges that moved the needle in our hearts for making foundational constraints. It has been said that those things that don't break you can only make you better. Well, I for one am living proof that those words ring ever true when it came to molding me into my adult life which was mostly a smooth transition from adolescence. Certainly, this was not because I had it figured out by any stretch or that challenges were not plenty, but mostly due to the fact that my future concerns of failing in the greater goals of life was creating in me a yearning to know how God's plan could help me get there. I desired to achieve things for me and my family in terms of financial and spiritual successes among others. I wanted to do it the faith way whereby creating a substantial basis for which we could always stay tethered in unmovable foundations. Many people today want to take shortcuts to get rich quick or to simply advance in some sort of facet but while those are noble ideas to be desired there is something to be said about taking the journey. I, for one, tried to take some short cuts along the way and I can assure you that for everyone that I thought would work most turned out to be dead ends or just simply unwise choices. In several cases, I had to ask God to help bail me out of these decisions and thankfully for those ones He had His grace available to me, yet some still had some unfavorable repercussions as a result.

So where is the fun you ask? As a multiple sport athlete in high school as well as being blessed to play collegiate baseball, I can tell you pretty much that numerous coaches which I was privileged to play under over these years would emphatically agree that the "Fun" definitely comes in the winning. I was able to be on teams where there was the thrill of victory and others that gave us the agony of defeat. Both scenarios required the same amount of effort when it came to development of athleticism and hours of practice for honing those skills necessary for a winning posture. Even still, with an ample amount of time and persistence you can find yourself on the losing end not because you were not prepared or good enough, but simply because someone was just better than you for that moment in time. I fully understand the feeling when athletes take losing to heart as so hurtful, but I have never understood the complete breakdown of character levied by an individual after a contest if you have given your best. One can only hope to do their best when the opportunity arises to meet a challenge. For believers in Christ, your best will never be enough to merit God's favor because of grace, yet you should always strive to offer Him your heart of excellence in everything you do. Scripture teaches that in everything you do in word or deed, do all for the glory of God for it is from Him that you receive the reward of your diligence. To bring it full circle in winning terms. Each of us are to do our best whether it's in parenting, marriage, friendships, or other endeavors that may seem insignificant in scope but have lasting effects on those who have relationships with us ongoing. The fun *will always be* found in the winning, but the winning will always be in doing your best before the Lord. God has never asked you or me to be perfect in who we are, although He does expect us to let Him perfect us into His image through Christ. My parents failed in many regards from a life measurement standard but because they did their best in their hearts for us relatively speaking, God was able to make His grace abound and pick up the pieces to cause all things to work for a greater good for me and my siblings.

He will do the same for you as well. Yes, I know we all fall short of his glory and that often times it means we sin against God in defiance or through ignorance but at the end of the day it's not what you did not do right that matters so much as where your heart resides in Christ. God by His Holy Spirit can convict you of wrong-doing faster and more expedient when you are toward Him in faith. Because He understands our humanity, He is still able to partner with us ongoing. The master of annoying love is Jesus Christ. He keeps coming for us all the time even when we resist His touch and turn away in emotional mannerisms and He will continue to do so. Falling down is less important than getting back up, so by continuing to walk in your faith and with determination to seek after God you will find His grace available which is what allows you the opportunity to grow up in Christ. These are the hallmarks of your biblical foundations. These are the ingredients of your stubborn faith which will become unyielding motivations that can be channeled through to the next generation as a model of consistency. We fall down, we get up! It's a Win-Win scenario to the faith minded. God working with you as Christ in you the hope of glory. An annoying love does not keep a score of losses earned nor does it record a losing season for posterity. It plays the game to win, and until your time runs out there is always a chance to score more wins. Dear friend, if you can keep the life game going along then you will be able to eventually achieve the foundational goals that you had purposed in your heart and mind for your family. Think about a time when you were playing a game like Monopoly. Early in the game maybe you got off to a bad start and kept landing on rents due or going to jail from chance cards. While it seemed like you should give up and quit the game, the tide of good fortunes can turn really fast in your favor once you began to dig in and start making purchases to help yourself all while other players get impacted just like you did. Yes, I know it's a game but from a comparative perspective it reflects real life because things can change swiftly to your detriment but praise God, things can also turn in your favor just as fast. For yourself, you have to make it real. You have to make it fun and to do so is to keep winning the good fight of faith. The Bible teaches that we will reap in due season if we do not faint and give up trying. Too many believers tend to give up easily and yield their spoils to the enemy without standing their ground and fighting for what is important to their faith. Your family is worth fighting for and you should do all you can to preserve their lives. If you do not do it for them, then who will? Someone took that stand for you to be where you are today. Maybe it was a hard road and maybe things were not good, but you made it regardless. Time to be a difference maker and time to be counted among the hall of faith achievers. You can make it happen and you will win, but never let quit get embedded in your moral fabric or it will be the Achilles heel of your faith in God.

If God said you can do all things in Christ, then it has been settled. Go and be a doer of the word.

Chapter Five – Assessing Where You Are Now

By now you should be getting the drift of what an annoying love is about and perhaps you are starting to make mental assertions regarding where you might be in the mix of your family's placement regarding this perspective. If so, then I have done what I intended from an initial standpoint and that is get your faith engine revved up enough to start assessing where you are now and what it will take to move you into this state of living the faith filled life at peak performance. But before we dive in, I would like to offer some transparencies from my own life that might help you to feel better and maybe not judge yourself too harshly if you feel like you've not measured well. As of this writing, my wife and I have successfully parented (relatively speaking, of course) and launched our four grown children. We have three boys and a girl, all of which have graduated from college, married, and have set their life careers in motion with half of them providing us with five wonderful grand babies. Along with our children, we also get four more additions to the family in three beautiful daughters-in-law and one awesome son-in-law. It's been amazing to see how our children have moved from the womb to the world in the past twenty plus years and we have often commented on how all of it seems to have passed in a blur. I mean really. It just feels like yesterday we were scrambling to keep diapers changed, food on the table, clothing supplied and in between school events or sport's teams among other things. These ventures just created more activities to be addressed while trying to find a landing place for serenity and sanity at days end. Whew! I just had a visual again, HA! Yes, it was hectic during those years but what part of parenting isn't when you do it fully involved?

If someone gave you a video of what your life would be like with children prior to having them, then perhaps you might choose to forgo it or reduce the number of children you wanted to have. In all honesty, we would not have traded them or those days for anything that might have brought us more financials rewards. Our greatest joys have come via being able to serve our immediate family as parents. But also and just as important, to be part of an enriched and expanded family community that got to participate in their lives throughout the past thirty plus years of our marriage. I can tell you without question that neither my wife nor myself had any inkling of how all this would work and turn out, but I will say that as committed believers in Christ we had a vision for what we had hoped for in the end. We just took living life one day at a time and fortunately the rest fell into place over the course of time. Our faith commitment and resolve to follow biblical standards were challenging for us as we had to wade through some turbulent waters and tall grasses of opposition over the years to keep us headed in the right direction. Sometimes, life seemed obscure in trying to take the path less traveled because in many cases we were plodding down a path that had no previous legacy markers for us to follow. Thanks be to God because He always made an illumination of His word as the light to direct our pathways. The challenges we faced were not new to God as so many saints have been there before but when it hits home for you and yours, you find that there was no precedent in your mindset to address it yet in God there was always a hope in faith. If anyone ever shares a boast in how they figured out all the stops during parenting years, then run away because either they are liars or pretenders. Everybody makes mistakes but you learn from experiences how to do better.

Part of the faith life is that you grow up in Christ by seeking, asking, and knocking on the doors of wisdom through utilizing the word of God, but also by exercising the applications of your knowledge as having obtained it in the quiet times of your devotions. The Church community is a great place to grow your faith as well as your family because it offers a laboratory of examples in demonstration and experience along with a practical teaching of resources made available on a routine basis. We were greatly blessed to have integrated into a local church body during those years that had a hunger for the things of God and pursued Him with a fervor that created a swell of passion for more than just a typical meeting place. The church people we became friends with for so many of these years as we reared our children together, both challenged and drew out of us elements of a Christian relationship that we had nurtured to employ for our family. It does take a village community to help raise a family. Some of those villagers are extended biological family, but many of those can and should also be the church family, community family, school family and yes even the social families. Each plays a role in helping to shape your parenting culture as they offer opinions and perspectives. Some are strangely different and sometime complex, but they help provide the iron elements to sharpen your spiritual tools so that they can become even better.

Many of these village groups we mentioned previously may actually be negative influences in nature or may provide contra positions to your faith beliefs. Even still you can use those as teaching examples for your children so that they get a stronger foundation to keep their hearts anchored. Of course, you will need to decide how often many of these people can affect your faith life and thus impact your family as result, so the onus will reside in your heart for letting this influence either shape you better or for worse. Ultimately, you are the captain of your family's faith vessel and charting your course can sometimes feel like you are mooring in darkness through a crashing sea of jagged rocks just waiting to do damage. As long as you keep your focus on the lighthouse [Jesus] you will get to your destination with everything still in the right place. It is true that we do need people in our lives, in our family, and in our communities. My wife and I encouraged them to be there for us as well as our children and embraced their value adding qualities to create a sense of social belonging but also confirm much of their spiritual growth acumen as a result of their friendship roles in building a family community.

Now that you get an idea of how to assess your state of the union regarding your family maybe you now have a slightly better feeling about it. To employ the annoying love in your faith walk as it relates to your family including your children is to realize that you have to measure the progress at all times. There is an assault on what you hold to be sound doctrine on so many sides and keeping on course has points of reference to adhere to. As I mentioned earlier regarding the village of communities necessary for raising a family, you should be aware that while this is necessary it can also be very confrontational as well as oppositional when it comes to your beliefs and foundations. You will be challenged at certain points in your journey by both family and friends to give an account for the hope of your calling in faith. In some cases, this will not go over well with those you are in relationships with. There were times when we had issues arise that created lost friendships or hurt feelings with family simply because we did not accept certain standards. While they were not necessarily bad influences, they were not things that we wanted to be a part of our family culture as an acceptable way of life. This does not mean that we were ultimately all right and they were all wrong, it just meant we had a different perspective in our faith convictions which we did not adhere to in the manner they may have. Simply put, agreeing to disagree. In some extreme cases, this can end up bringing about separation because reconciliation cannot be bridged by the two strong opposing opinions. Sometimes a separation of relationship may have to work its way out but there's hope to revive it in the future too.

Likewise, you are score keeper in your family's faith and the word of God should be your measuring stick. As you are assessing where you stand within your household of faith be sure to know what your core values are, what your family vision or mantra is, and how do you want to posture your home for Christ. I would wager that most people haven't taken the time to consider these three elements, but I would argue that unless you want to get to your intended destination you have to begin with the end in mind. Our family vision was simple- Live, Love, and Laugh. Yeah, I know you can find this motto this on most home décor items at Kirkland's or At Home stores, but we were original in this thought before they coined it on a sign. Of course we had an expanded version of those three words which had relevance to our home but that was the simple way to keep it before us. If you keep your assessment simple and basic, then you can allow for growth and modification of some ideas as your children begin to participate in this as well. However, the caution again is to make sure it's in agreement with the word of God and is not carried away with a secular or social society agenda. In our modern world today we find so much acceptance and adherence to truths that are not biblical but rather socially acceptable to fit a narrative for cultural influences. As parents, you must guard your children's hearts and minds on a daily basis because this can be the breeding ground for creating foundational cracks in your family's Christian faith. Remember that a little leaven will leaven the whole lump. It doesn't take much for the divisive intrusion to begin breaking down those things which you have held in check. A little compromise here and there in your course direction and soon you will be drifting into a place that gets you off the right pathway and into another position that can shudder your vision. Routine checkups are required to address your family's spiritual needs, but the good news is you have many resources available. As we discussed previously, the church can help be a pulse for your faith endeavors but ultimately prayer, reading and sharing the word of God with each other will do more usually than those things could do. It helps tremendously to develop a listening heart for the voice of the Lord. What an amazing way to build your child's faith than to teach them to listen to the voice of the Good Shepherd and shut down the noise from all of the other voices making sounds all around. What we yield in one generation we reap in another so it is important to hold fast to the confessions of our faith and believe God will sustain us as we walk in obedience to His word.

To reiterate, the love that parents will demonstrate to their family will seem annoying in many cases, but it will be the very element to help redeem them just as God did for us through giving Jesus Christ. Having reached the end of our parenting journey as far as being their mom and dad in our home as authority figures, it gives us great joy in knowing that we were able to build their foundation faith. While they are now solely responsible, at least we can cling to the Proverb that admonishes us to train them up in the way they should go and when they are older, they will have the means to return to it. God doesn't have grandchildren in the faith and each generation has to purpose to choose Him for their lives. If we can set the tone and establish the parameters, we have a hope in God that this establishment will reap benefits for their salvation. You are only required to be stewards and to be obedient in your faith as parents or family leaders. As scriptures remind us that in the faith walk some plant, some water, but God gives the increase when it comes to redemption. We are held accountable for the stewardship of our children as parents and although they are gifts given initially to us to manage in faithful living, we will be required to present them back to God as good gifts for his Kingdom. This is a process to help them fulfill their purposes in life according to the word of the Lord, so we must answer the call to the fullest degree and without restraint. Amos chapter three asks the question can two people walk together except they be agreed? Without a doubt the emphatic answer is no so make sure everyone is on the same page at all times and things will go much better.

Chapter Six – Breaking Down Barriers

In Ephesians chapter six, Paul deals with the weapons of our spiritual warfare that have been made available to us through God and how He has fully equipped us through the Holy Spirit to win the good fight of faith. The listing of the warrior's equipment consistent within this passage has been specifically designed to provide an assortment of battle armor that will handle the onslaught of an invisible enemy yet does not offer any defense for rear protection. From the top of our head to the tip of our toes we have been given strategic battle elements which are inlaid with the power of God's word. This supplies the necessary and adequate clothing to make sure our defensible capabilities are more than enough to position us as being beyond a conqueror for warfare. What we discover within the context of this writing is that we as believers were designed and given the task for advancing the Kingdom yet without a retreating opportunity of any proportion. Scripture teaches that the Kingdom of light suffers the attacks of violence but the righteous take it head on by force. Therefore, the understanding is that we go into battle and God is our shield and defender such that we will not face a fear of being assaulted at our rear guard because our God is a shield about us and the glory and lifter of our head. In other words, God has our backs at all times, but He has equipped us to advance against the gates of hell and we will prevail because the battle is the Lord's when we take up arms for His Kingdom's purpose. Too many believers fail at the idea of battle because of their timidity in knowing that our God is able. He has not given us over to a spirit of fear, but one of superior power, love, and a sound mind of understanding. Oh what a joy to have received this understanding regarding the word of the

Lord in your devotional times which is ever paramount to equipping yourself for daily battle.

It is through this battle mentality that we must come to understand that we are in a fight. Not just a good fight of faith, but an unfair fight of preference with God as the trump card. You see we have God in us the hope of glory and this power incarnate through Christ Jesus as our savior empowers us to triumph over ALL things. Jesus stated for the early disciples that all power in heaven and earth has been given unto Him, and with that same manifested presence He has yielded this Word sword for us as born-again believers to both embrace and enact in our faith walk. Jesus didn't just die and be resurrected for our ticket to get punched on our journey to heaven. Not at all. He went down to the enemy's camp and took back the keys to death, hell, and the grave so we could understand resurrection power at his peak performance when we exercise our faith as well. We have been given all the weapons we need to activate the spiritual defense system, and so many times we forget that it is not a carnal battle but mighty through God for the pulling down of strongholds. The struggles we face in this realm are not with our flesh and blood family or friends, although often times it may resemble them, but with rulers and authorities in high places of power having been given an evil force by these powers of darkness. They are real and they are relevant in this modern age. Yet, just as Jesus stepped up and resisted the devil in His forty days of temptations while fasting and developing His faith walk, we have that same power available to us that raise Christ from the dead to quicken us daily. We should practice that strategy in the same way as he did.

To understand this Spiritual posturing of faith and how it affects our family is to know that there is an enemy prowling about seeking to devour every facet of family life with a chip on his shoulder to do harm to your household foundations. If he can penetrate even one area of your faith covenants, then he can gain access to your children in sordid ways that leave lasting impacts. But do not fear! You have the ability and the priority from God's word to keep him at bay and push back the gates of hell so that they will not prevail against you. You can break down barriers or roadblocks in your family life that prevent an acceleration of growth and commitment to Christ for each generation. This allows you to create a legacy of faith for promoting the gospel across these future generations. Sometimes, we only think about tearing down barriers that bring separation from things or persons that were maybe racially motivated or perhaps prejudiced due to a certain walk of life. These definitely should be torn down. We also need to know that those spiritual barriers of fear, doubt, and unbelief get cemented in families through traditions past down from well meaning "faith advisors" who have limited exposure to scripture. For whatever reason their interpretations determine that their doctrine is the standard. The problem is that while they may be faithful in their gospel commitment and have limited Bible knowledge, their spiritual growth could be stagnant simply because they have never been stretched in faith endeavors. I digress here, but I'm reminded of a comedy movie once that had a well-known punch line when the family was getting together for a holiday and issues were happening. As a result some members of the family wanted to keep it a secret so as to not let the rest of its family know any different what was going on. Kind of a cover up or keeping it under the radar to put it mildly. The family patriarch finally spoke up having been the instigator and simply stated after conferring the agreed upon decision, "Well I guess it's true that you can't spell families without lies." Unfortunately, this is true in many cases either by a choosing or not, but we can change this tone by challenging the narratives.

Now I'm not saying you need to avoid or dismiss these people altogether, but as the battle has intensified for your family's foundations, it is imperative that parents grow a greater faith measure beyond the last generation. This doesn't imply that they were inferior in their walk. However, it does mean that each generation should learn to stand on the shoulders of the previous generation and purpose to increase the magnitude of their faith walk. Parents especially have a responsibility to be better than their parents as each legacy has to keep repairing the breaches which take impacts from the battle that rages forward from generation to generation. The invisible enemies give no slumber to their plans and assault but thankfully God is always aware of their schemes and is providing us a heads-up mentality through the Holy Spirit. Don't feel in the least bit overwhelmed or intimidated because of the spiritual war that is going around you but take courage in knowing God has made provisions for His own to be victors. Those barriers can and will come down, but we have to be diligent in our efforts. Sometimes for parents this tenacity is met with opposition by our children because they have little understanding of what we inherently know is going on around us. In their mind all they want is to be able to do their own thing. My wife and I dealt with this attitude on many occasions from our children who couldn't understand our perspective ultimately and maybe we were too strict or discerning regarding some matters. In hindsight, we erred on the side of what we sensed in our hearts at that stage of our children's life. Sometimes you just have to do things because you know that you know it is the right approach. This often times means you can't explain a reasonable why to your children, but you shoulder an annoying love mentality that this is the way were going to play it because this is the way we see it in our mind's eyes. Mature parents understand this and when their kids finally reach a certain place in life where they have that same position, it usually dawns on them that they too have to play the same tough love roles and make the hard decision to the chagrin of their family.

In these scenarios like begets like, and faith produces more faith. But not just a same faith. Better faith. Stronger faith. Strategic faith. Faith that prevails and protects. Faith that raises a standard and triumphs over the evil assault on the foundational truths that have been placed in the walls of your household and will give your home a quality of life needed for growing your children to win at the next level of their faith walk. There is no substitute to removing those barriers that hinder biblical growth in God and rightly so. No one can do what you are called to do as a parent, and nothing else can be the light you are to your world. We all have a role to play and as we equip ourselves daily, we have the capacity to equip others with us along the same pathway. Mom and Dad. You are the salt of the family world so you cannot allow your spiritual seasoning to be lost in your household. You are the light set on a hill of fatherhood and motherhood whose brightness has to be shown so that God's narrow path can be seen by your children vividly and faithfully every day. While this may seem heavy, it is not so much in a relative parental application. You have the necessary anointing because of your faith status in having partnered through a creative work with God, with all His resource credentials available in all circumstances. So be encouraged knowing that the same opportunities you will face have been seen by multitudes across the millennia. While each one is different in its context, there remains that God will allow His grace to abound to you, so you always will have His sufficiency for every good work. Parenting is a good work and you have chosen well to shoulder this in loving a life.

Chapter Seven – Equipping the Clan

I'm a big college football fan and have tendencies to watch more games than I should during the fall season each year. I have such a penchant to really keep a pulse on what other teams are doing well in comparison to my favorite team, and how it will all work out for us as we approach the championship stretch. Yeah, I know but it's hard to not do this at times seeing how I used to play sports and football was one of my favorites along the way. Part of the sports viewership exercise requires one to take liberties to assess your favorite team as an armchair quarterback. Everyone does it in some form or fashion whether it's found from a sports perspective or just in general as a common practice related to any matters of conversation. We may not spend enormous efforts addressing those concerns with significant others like we should. However, we do hold these thoughts in our minds as to how hindsight could have been a major tool for replaying the episode in a better or more expediate fashion. As a parent, we often have these conscious epiphanies for what we could have done better when it came to a disciplinary venture or perhaps even a better solution for how we chose to play a certain role of development for our children. No doubt we could always do better if we had the "do-over" opportunity available like we do with a replay button on the remote, or in film study if you happen to be a coaching professional. At the end of the day, the overarching reality is you have to do your best at that moment in time and hope that your decision was best thought out long before you had the demands to make a choice. Early preparation is always the best time before the event comes to fruition to be rolling over ideas and consequential outcomes so that you don't find yourself being blasted into making a poor choice simply because you get caught off guard. Sure that sounds logical but not always practical since we rarely ever get a heads up in life impacting moments. But just what if you did? Would that make you better, smarter, or even wiser? Maybe or maybe not? Still, the more we can prepare ourselves and our hearts before the storm the less often we have to repair for collateral damages in the end.

What is true though can be found in the fact that no matter how hard you try or how much you prepare there will always be something in life to "one up" your preparation and planning but those are the exceptions and not the rule. For now though, you have a great opportunity to deal with the routines and learn to be consistent in your parenting as well as everything else you do on a consistent basis. As it stands, most children find comfort and safety in home environments that lend itself to steadiness and uniformity with occasional moments of spontaneity that promotes fun and creativity. In other words, you might have a predictable nature to your life and living but there needs to be some zestfulness of development in order to move your family forward without stagnation. To be an equipper in any format requires a lot of energy and flexibility such that you don't exasperate the persons for whom you are helping in the growth process. Life coaches have become a big deal in the modern world today because they are strategic influencers who have achieved the fine art of mentoring others. They have persona of creating dynamics that keep their valuation of encouragement front and center. Mom and dad, all is not lost in any hope you have to keep your children's attention and devotion, but I can tell you that one must work at it daily. You are competing in today's culture with so many outside influences that are vying for your children's attention and your placement of character faces an uphill climb almost daily. The good news is that you have the ultimate opportunity to lay the faith foundational groundwork early on and support it with continual spiritual development everyday of their life.

I fully agree that it is overwhelming at times to compete with all the noises they have been introduced to as impressionable youth, but if you begin setting the tone and managing the influences in your home then you can build a guard over their hearts. Your role is not to isolate them from all harm but rather to insulate their life in such a way that they understand what it means to be protected yet perfected for Christian living. My wife and I tried to create a realistic life posture when dealing with our children allowing them to understand and experience firsthand what both sides of the coin would look like if flipped either way. To our children we were definitely annoying in our love approach as we took measures to be in their lives strongly in ways to build that life hedge of faith around them. They did not like it most times and even expressed resistance to our demands. The result was that we won out on the positions that mattered spiritually not because we were unreasonable, but because we were united in setting the tone of our household. Parents this is a necessary application you must embrace, and it has to be an anchor of daily living else you find your foundations starting to crumble beneath the assaults that will be levied in their life for compromising your beliefs. I'm sad to say that I've witnessed other parents whose children were friends of ours cave into to those demands simply because they were trying to be their friend and not their parent. Listen closely parents and leaders. You are not positioned to be their friend in parenting from birth to adolescence! You are there to be a person of authority, guidance, and correction to lead them forward into battle yet with a heart of love and respect. A Marine First Sergeant when taking on new inductees is not interested in being a friend to the recruits, but rather in building and bending their wills so that they understand what it means to be led in getting equipped for battle. Doesn't mean you have to be a hard-hearted tyrant by any stretch, but you do have to know your role and play it fully for them to get it. Tough love sometimes has to take place when it comes to discipling others for the Kingdom. The neat thing is, once you bridge that endeavor it makes crossing over each time a lot less difficult because you have set a cadence that your children will learn to walk to throughout their time in your home. As they grow and mature into adulthood, you will be able step away from that strong parenting role and into the friendship zone to both enjoy and employ life choices for the grandparenting years ahead. We are enjoying some of those fruits today as we are watching our children developing their own unique parenting roles for our grandchildren and we hide the smiles on our faces knowing that they have exhibited some of our parenting tendencies. However, each one has begun to exercise their own special processes as well as they build their faith houses.

The book of Ephesians talks about equipping the saints for the work of the ministry by incorporating the five-fold ministry of the mature spiritual believers into the local church. This adds value but it also allows diversity and creativity to be implemented to all believers where they can find the resources for growing their faith beyond just their own philosophy of knowledge. As a parent, you are an equipper of faith! You have been given the task of building leaders, along with mentoring men and women who will one day take their places among the saints to pass the baton for future generations. As you set the standards, build the fortifications, and display that faith before them on a daily basis they will learn to embrace and reflect that nature of God because we have a promise to assure us. It doesn't always happen on our time, but it will happen in time so don't despair or fret. Equipping your clan can take time and effort. Jacob who became Israel had a big family clan and while these young men were the eventual patriarchs of our faith as leaders of tribes, early on they were liars and deceivers who tried to destroy one of their own brothers. God always has a plan and just like he used their wrong doings to bring about righteous endings so will he keep your family in the same way. Be bold and courageous and understanding that your family and your future generations are depending on you doing your part. We all have to partner with God in creation to bring children into the world, but we also have to continue that mantra in order for them to be made complete and equipped. Your clan is not any different from anyone else's clan. They all need a strong family bond that is tethered to the faith of a Christian foundation. When you build this in your home you are breaking ground and setting the stones in place for hope in the future. Thus, it becomes more important and necessary for parents in continuing to build upon it as life moves ahead for your family growth.

From Abraham to Isaac to Jacob who then eventually became Israel to their God, there was always a passing of the baton to the next generation for not only understanding the significant roles to play but also in comprehending the detrimental outcomes should they fail in their pursuits. While this First Family of Faith had many failings and shortcomings within their lineage, they all portrayed the attributes of faithfulness in a covenant relationship God had setup for them to succeed in. This faith was cast into a foundational mantra which carried our biblical landscape beyond the religious caricature which continues to try and align itself within the gospel framework of modern Christianity. We must strive to preserve the Christian elements for which the church society has flourished in while adhering to the standards of God's word with unwavering resolve. Our present and future family clans will demand nothing more so we must give nothing less than a full commitment to our Lord Jesus Christ always. Your clan is your plan for the future of a family's posterity as well as the space capsule for launching faith into the next generation as a better way of living life. The Bible has a hodgepodge of unique and dissimilar storylines that follow paths of family disfunction, but their end game seems to always bring them back to a rightful position of being in God's service no matter how they journey in disarray. It's not unlike many strange things we see today in this modern age of anything goes. Be encouraged to know that God still knows how to maneuver people throughout the changing times of culture, and he still allows his truth to become relevant in every generation even when it seems faith has lost its spiritual grip.

Chapter Eight – Your Recipe for Success

I like to cook different things in our kitchen from time to time and consider myself adept at figuring out how to make certain tasty dishes either by trial and error, or sometimes just by checking out a magazine example or perhaps a social media posting of one. Now I have to also admit that I sometimes hit on a tasteless dud. I either didn't listen well enough on the preparation and failed to use the right ingredients included, or I simply just winged it hoping for the best because I was in too big of a hurry. Understand that my desire to make the supper meal moment a big success for my wife and I can be undermined very easily at the cost of shortcuts and miscalculations on my part. The sad note is that if I would have simply followed the baking guidelines that someone took the time to list, then I would have had a far greater chance of being successful in my cuisine endeavors. This is my main excuse for not baking cakes or pastries since it requires me to stick to the recipes and I have the tendency to go off the grid which is bad in the end. So I stay more on the barbeque and grilling opportunities which afford me latitude in cooking. So what does this have to do with building the annoying love mentality you ask? Great questions so let's dive into the mix.

First, just like a great dinner requires adequate preparation and right ingredients to create a masterpiece dish that everyone rants about and wants seconds, so we must understand that there is a necessary recipe for success in building a faith family. I want to establish here that a faith family is not equal to a religious family. While the two have certain aspects and attributes which weave and web together in some of their religious expressions, the truth is there are distinct ingredient differences in the two and must be understood just as a biscuit and brisket have their own distinct tastes. Religion in its purest form is a reflective element of ascribing homage to God from a standoff distance perspective, while not necessarily attending to Him in a self-expression of the heart. In other words, it's a ritualistic display act with hopes of acknowledging a God on a recognitional pathway yet not allowing the pursuant the experience or the full exercise of addressing God through personal relationships. To describe it in the food terms I've been addressing previously, it would be like buying a can of pre-made biscuits to prepare and bake in the oven for a quick meal. I'm not knocking this food choice as I have had my share of these prefabbed pucks over the years. Even though you participated in opening the bag or can in order to place these biscuits on a cooking sheet to put in the oven, the fact remains that you only followed directions, so you did not have an active participation in the biscuit creative process. Unfortunately, many people today are trading true worship for watching performers sing and celebrate and leave their local service still not impacted or changed. In fact, many services have morphed into fast food cultures where the Pastors have to make ready to go combos of sermons that quickly inspire patrons. If this can't be handled well enough, they'll find their congregations splitting across the county to form coffee house style venues where people can feel better engaged about their church experience. Creativity in reaching others in faith circles can be helpful as well as harmful.

For the record, I'm not against creating more of a culture or allowing opportunities to exist inside the church buildings for the people's social needs. Just know that we should not be trying to make the church look like Starbucks or the RPX Movie Theater just so people will come because it has a cool vibe. Having been in ministry for over thirty years in pastoral and administration roles, I can tell you that leaders are always looking to invest and invite outsiders to attend while hoping to close the back door for those looking for better things elsewhere. The key to this, I believe, is found in creating the faith culture and that starts at home and not in the local church. Yes, the church should carry the torch for building and augmenting a family's spiritual needs weekly and I have been blessed to attend ones that do just that. But if we are giving too much credence to what we think people will like versus what God wants, then we have veered off course. We may find the great continental faith drift happening in the church and as such it will creep into the home as well. The right recipe for building strong faith families should be undergirded by building right minded churches who have the benchmark foundations of a concrete spirituality which should be developed in the home ongoing by the leaders of the family unit. The families are the cultural influence for giving churches a spiritual bull's eye approach.

Case in point: For decades we have relied on the government to teach and educate our children with our tax dollars which to a small degree worked somewhat well during the sixties to eighties decades because parents were involved jointly in supporting this concept. Since then there have been less participation by moms and dads to help learning. Some of these have been due to multiple wage earner jobs, divorce issues that separate kids from parents, or just a lack in supporting education as well as helping with additional homework to enhance academic learning. The results of this shift has led to our nation falling behind in educational excellence creating its own list of problems from poverty to literacy. My point is that as parents we have to rebuild some of the faith stones that have been torn down by cross cultural ideas. Yes, we should be ever changing and reinventing new ways of doing things better and with more impact, but our Christian foundations for sound biblical home life has to be a priority first by the parents. These same parents are leaders in the church, communities and in businesses where their influences can shape the next generations for Christ. We have lost vision for this as anti-God socially culture minded agendas have begun to rob us of our moral values for the nation we once embraced in God. Thus, our children are the ones who will face picking up the fragmented pieces. Think about how much the church has changed in the past twenty years. More growth has occurred in its building construction, technology, professionalism and in its socialization endeavors than in really developing and discipling believers. Sure the App platforms allow for advancement and exposure today through social media, but the fact remains that we know more about Bible things and have access to spiritual media, yet we love less in our actions toward others. We spend more time on matters of what is being discussed to like it or hate it on practically any subject, but we spend so little time now on what matters most and that is people's hearts and lives. Our children are facing more bullying, more suicides, more drugs, more hate, more of everything and as parents we gave them these social media or "smart phone" tools to help them have better lives. Apparently, we are the Not-So-Smart ones after all since this moved the needle in the wrong direction when it comes to boosting their faith walk with Christ.

Moms and dads let's take back the ground that we yielded to the enemy and be more supportive of our children's hearts than we are their social preferences. I remember when our children were in high school and mobile phones were taking off with kids needing to have them for certain reasons of school or to be in communication with their parents. Now it seems parents communicate less with them because their children's time is spent following everyone but God and it's no one's fault but our own. We can redeem the time! We can change the narrative! It will have some painful hiccups in the process but just know that your children's faith depends on it and their hearts are hungry for it. There is a middle ground to meet with your clan on what matters most in the home, but it has to be solid ground that has a spiritual foundation as the bedrock in order for it to hold strong against the attacks. Every child wants to feel loved, protected, and safe in their home life knowing that there is always a shelter from the storms of life. Parents hold in their hand the umbrellas of faith that need to be raised and opened so their children can see it always available to them when the rain falls hard. It does rain on the just and the unjust, but I believe they will come and get out of the storm so that your love will be as a protective blanket of comfort to them from time to time. Don't be dismayed as they will show strong resistance at various times in life, especially as they approach puberty with hormones and temptations raging inside. However, the annoying love of a mom or dad can overcome all their conflicting mind-sets. We have to keep doing the deal over and over again to make it stick and to make it real enough for them to catch the drift. Some things need to be caught as well as taught for it to have a lasting effect! We have to follow the full gospel recipe to the utmost measure so that we know what we can expect from them. Parenting adolescent children is not the time to step out and do your own adult thing while letting the tweeners figure it out themselves. Parent, maybe you as a teenager had to figure things out yourself because your parents spent your pre-adult life taking advantage of their freedom from diapers and daycares to discover themselves again, but you have to finish the journey. Yes, parents should make time for themselves to have moments for living their life together as adults, but not at the expense of their children's spiritual welfare. Moms and dads have to keep towing the line daily so that no slack can get built up within the family faith and create bottlenecks of spiritual deficiency that serve as nooses to bind their children's growth and maturity.

The creators of great cuisine dishes spend time to perfect the ingredients needed to ensure that their platters of provision taste delicious enough to capture it as a recipe for others to share. Why would you as a parent or family leader do any less when it comes to your household? As a faith person you embody the spiritual ingredients necessary to mold and shape your family into becoming a God focused and Christ centered home. The Bible contains all the recipes of life you'll ever need for you to utilize growth within your family, plus the Holy Spirit will be your chief cook to guide and keep the pulse on when to add the next ingredient to make your children into the gift they are to become. Stay the course and follow the recipe of success and you will discover the joys of a well done good and faithful servant mantra bidding from the Lord! We all should understand that life is about stewardship and even the Apostle Paul described it as a requirement to be found faithful in managing one's affairs. How great will it be to get the God seal of approval over our lives in so many facets of service opportunities and in particular as it relates to our children's hearts. The neat thing is if we are doing the necessary due diligence in managing our hearts before the Lord, then carrying it over into our family life as well. Within our friendship circles it helps us to establish that annoying love attitude which easily gets scattered throughout the course of our existence without huge efforts on our part. Just like you get better at making certain dishes the more you frequent the preparation and cooking of them, you become more instinctive in applying the right amounts of ingredients for building the family faith. You then know what it takes more of and now you have assurance that it will all work out according to God's ultimate plan for your household.

Chapter Nine – Being Involved Is a Good Thing

No doubt raising a God-fearing Christ-centered family today is a monumental task for even the best of faith-based families who have a lineage and generational heritage of Christian commitment. One thing is still certain, there are no grandchildren in the Kingdom of Heaven as each individual member must be born again in their heart and receive the grace of salvation through the cross of Christ. This purposes that every person born into this world has the human choice and free will for their life once they reach the age of accountability to choose a path that will lead to heaven or hell. Many critics today would argue that there is no hell, but scripture makes it completely clear that to be absent from the body is to either be present with God in Heaven or spend an eternity in hell tormented as a result of not receiving the pardon of sin found only in Jesus. My point being that it is imperative that parents keep building the foundations of Christian living so that their children will desire to choose that narrow path as they move forward in their understanding of who God is and how they can participate in a relationship with him. It's so fun to see young children especially little ones all dressed up in outfits that look similar to mom or dad's attire and in their young hearts they want to be just like them at least for a short season. Of course, we understand that is short lived until they hit a certain stage in life, but the sincerity and innocence of their desire at that moment is beyond special to a parent. I remember my daughter at a very young age telling me that she wanted to marry me one day and as a dad it can really melt your heart quickly. Of course, our sons did the same thing toward my wife, and she still makes mention of it to their embarrassed grins today as married adults. The real takeaway is that in their innocence they saw something of value that encouraged their hearts to want to be a part of and that element was unconditional love given toward them.

We understand our children won't always like what we like or want things like we do, but that window is available for short time, and we need to help them fill up their love buckets with the right things. The fact that they try to copy us at a young age shows how impressionable their hearts are but also how influential their minds can be. In our thirty plus years of parenting our four children, I would estimate that the optimum influencing window to be from birth to around eight years of age with much of that being stronger just before five years of age, so it's a great chance to really cover some ground. The unique opportunity we found that gave us an advantage was with my wife homeschooling them for a good decade of time. Because of her commitment to teach them, she helped to shape their hearts both educationally as well as academically which added more influence for our role modeling capability. I realize everyone can't do homeschooling as it was a stretch for my wife to work parttime as a nurse and still hold to commitments, but she was a major reason they achieved education well when it came time to enroll them in public school. I like to take credit as the PE teacher and sports coach, but the truth is they went farther in academics than sports, although it did help some to make them more well-rounded. We also utilized our local church resources that were available for music and fine arts, homeschool cooperatives as well as other activities that helped influence them for Christ centered learning. At the time they were really engaged and participated in plays, choirs, and social retreat activities but as they matured these things became less of an influence, so we knew it was time to translate them to a different avenue of learning in public education. While they were eager to spread some wings and find new friends and activities, we continued to keep a close pulse on their hearts and lives as far as what they could or could not do as it related to our core values. This is where the annoying love mantra became a reality to both them and us. While they pushed back against us to gain some exposure and freedoms, we kept the lines of communication and commitments tethered to our faith home. They knew what the limitations were ongoing. We were far from perfect in our parenting endeavors and I'm sure that each of our children would share their stories of disdain and heartburn because of our modeling, but at the end of your parenting journey you have to account for how you choose to raise them.

We chose to be in their space as often as we could and to be in their face time daily as real and open in terms of how things were happening around them, as we had a relative sense of where they were. We were not helicopter parents but probably more like drones keeping surveillance on the state of the family yet continuing to support both family and faith as it related to their lives. We were probably overbearing to hear them speak about it today and maybe in hindsight we were somewhat that. Though, I believe they now understand why we became the parents to them we tried to be in order to guard their hearts. We were involved in all aspects of their life more as it related to just being mom and dad simply because we had such a passionate love for them and wanted to spend as much time as we could to support the things that they valued. Some of the things you do, the places you go, and the activities you allow participation in are all part of building their hearts for Christ. An annoying love can be a two-sided coin where you have to give in an abundance of love in order to get specific results you have hoped for as a spiritual leader. Parenting will always have some bartering of exchange elements in it because as parents you are growing together a framework and each child requires a different measure of attention and discipline in order to round off the rough edges. Some of the attributes that you as a spiritual leader learned from your parents may or may not play a role in how you handle certain things within your household. However, I believe each of us can learn to utilize previous generation examples to help us make our own tools sharper. We should look to cherry pick the things of yester year which have real life values that fit into our spiritual core today and refresh those in new creative ways. The one major attribute that we employed was to be involved in the lives of our children from sunrise to sunset on a daily basis. My dad earned his living being gone off to work for weeks at a time and while he loved to be a part of our sports activities when he was around, the truth is he missed out on much of the routine opportunities as a result of his vocation. His focus was on provision for our humble home, and he sacrificed what he knew to do to make it happen. Parents sometimes have to make the hard but necessary decisions on what is priority and what is preferred. They are not mutually inclusive choices.

For us, we chose to sacrifice personal preferences so we could be available and assessable to our family for as long as we had them at home with us. We worked our vocations and provided a living to meet our family's needs. We also took time to enjoy the small things in life like a park-nic lunch on vacation, a weekly pizza buffet outing for the homeschoolers, and sometimes just a good ole wrestling moment in the floor with me being ganged up on by the kids. *Note to parents:* Playroom wrestling is only good until they are able to jump off the couch in unison and inflict pain on dad, lol. Being involved in your child's life is probably the most important aspect of parenting beyond the spiritual development that must take place in order to have the faith-based family atmosphere. Your children need to have your time as well as your resources because that is what builds their character and shapes their hearts for future generational conveyance. Children will find it hard to understand how much you love them unless you demonstrate it on a routine basis. I understand certain professions require a large amount of time or commitment for earning a living, but you have to find those windows of connection to fill up their love buckets as they will run dry if left unchecked. As a general rule, make it a priority to build in times for gathering and be strategic as to when these will be so everyone has the expectation of what is important to them. As a kid growing up with my siblings, we rarely had vacation times of going away together due to finances or other reasons, but as a parent we made and still make this a priority to get away with our family as often as we can afford. Now that they are grown and on their own, they still love to go with mom and dad on trips and have adopted this decision as part of their own families as well. I get some flack each year about planning trips mostly to use our timeshare, but in the end, it seems to do the trick quite well. Although I readily admit I need to start picking some new places to visit now that they are adults with grandchildren and new interests of their own. We all know habits are vices, but change is not change until you change it. I'm working on changing but I do like my Go-To places.

There's a T-shirt company that has a slogan (Life is Good) which has a stick cartoon figure on it and is easily recognizable if you've ever shopped at a retail store that has them available. The truth is life is good because God is good. Things may not be as good as they could be, should be, or you hoped they would be, but when we recognize our privileged position in life as a parent, we should be glad it is as good as it is. We don't get to choose what kind of children we will have, but we do get to determine how we will raise them as it relates to the gifts we are given from God. They are a prize and blessed is the man whose quiver is full them as the Psalmist wrote. Contrary to some thoughts today, children are not a burden in any way shape or form. A growing sentiment in the modern age is that kids are selfish to steal your time, energy, and resources so you should limit your number when having them or have none at all. My wife and I never really sat down and said we will have four children when we began our life journey together, but once they started being born into our lives, we could not have imagined how special they were and how blessed we are. In fact, we thought perhaps we should have had more but now that the grands are here, we take joy in being able to spoil them and give as much love away as we can. The good news for us is found in the next generation as our grandchildren offer us the simple pleasure of seeing our family expand exponentially without having to be directly responsible for raising them. We do get to augment their lives as part of the grand village of in-laws. What a joy to have your own children and be a part of stewarding them into adult life, and then watching them step up to become parents themselves who embody the characteristics of multiple family generations because of their union in God. I have had the privilege of seeing my children come to Christ through our spiritual home of influence, been able to baptize them in their faith acknowledgment through the local church, and then charge them forward as an officiator of their marriage vows before the Lord. Funny, my dream for my life was to have played Major League Baseball when I entered collegiate athletics after high school, but along the way God had a much better plan to let me be blessed beyond measure. As scripture can often remind one if we let it, that the mind of a man plans his thoughts, but it is the Lord who orders his pathway. I'm glad I was willing to let God reorder my plans and give me a heritage of faith to pass forward. My hope is that you too will be willing to allow God entrance into your heart and life, and that making your family home one of faith and focus on the Lord Jesus Christ will more than give you fulfillment for generations to come. There's not a greater accomplishment in being a parent than seeing your children launch into new horizons knowing they have the right stuff inside of their heart. If they choose to follow it then their lives will know God's blessings as well. Of course, it's up to them choosing to follow God, but we can have some assurance that if we train them in the way they should go forward in life, that when they become older, they will return to this faith-based way of living. Unfortunately, God doesn't give a timeframe on when this will happen in their lives, but He does give us a word of faith promise.

Parents and family leaders, your involvement is paramount to succeeding by making your home the safe haven of refuge and renewal. There are no shortcuts to achieving your ultimate family's objective because faith always demands the very best of your character, your excellence as well as your full-fledged commitment to its calling. Yes, God is present with you at all times doing His part, but never forget that there will always be a "your part" requirement. He will not do what He has orchestrated for you to complete as part of your destiny to be established in a lasting achievement heritage. As long as you and your loving spouse partner to embrace this challenge and pursue it with a vengeance of strong convictions, there can be a great hope for achieving these expectations. The good news is God doesn't expect perfection from us, but He will always require faithfulness and obedience to His word as we journey forward in the faith of building families for Christ. In today's world, it often requires a lot of effort to make success so many different things, but parents must find creative ways to plug into the child's life for the important moments as these will build hearts of remembrance. My wife and I had to be very intentional in many aspects of our living in order to carve out avenues of support so that our children recognized our commitment to them was without question and with an all-in heart.

Chapter Ten – Fingerprinting Your Family

Just like every criminal mystery novel has a defined and elaborate story plot within its text to ultimately lead the reader into finding out who is responsible for the crime, there will always be the proverbial smoking gun as to where blame or innocence will rest. With any investigative detective work performed there will ultimately be the one true outlier that brings the connection point of cause and effect together. This leaves little doubt as to the questioning of its results. That one selective item will always be the very fingerprint left in the wake of activity that leads others back to the one responsible for the outcomes of either carnage or homage. In the case of a faith family, this will in fact be prevalent throughout the years of rearing your children as they will become the impressionable character person that parents will stamp emphatically with their spiritual ink blotter. Having been in financial arenas as part of my professional business acumen, I can certify without a doubt that ink pads or mechanical ink stampers can leave a lasting imprint on one's skin, albeit a short timeframe if left in the wake of their errant use. However, this ink obviously and eventually will fade due to its chemical nature but rest assured that the indelible spiritual mark you will place upon your family as a believer will remain with them far longer that your lifetime and will ultimately endure to continue into future generations as well if done correctly. Thus, the imprint process has been set in motion ongoing for the family.

To continue the crime analogy, a good detective, after determining who their key suspect is, will find sustainable evidence so he can obtain an arrest warrant to bring the alleged perpetrator in for booking as a means to pursue their ultimate objective. In this process a fingerprinting establishment has now taken place and will create a long-standing measure of record for future identification purposes. Parents, you have this same fingerprinting opportunity within the confines of their Christian family household. This can create lasting impressions not only in a life reflective of their core values, but also one that is expressed by a heart yielded to the power of the Holy Spirit. Not enough of this has been passed forward in many modern-day homes and as such it has left a huge spiritual void for so many in recent generational cultures. You, as a parent or leader in the home, have the unique opportunity to refresh the mentality and mindset of very impressionable people who will become tomorrow's world changers. What an awesome chance to pay it forward for future generations and set a gospel tone that endures beyond the family name. It then becomes dedicated to promoting Christ in the marketplace as well as in the church. Understanding that, your children need what you have to offer them in the way of spiritual development even though their young ages don't allow them to articulate it in simple terms. The needs facing many today are still basic concepts that will elevate their hearts beyond the basic necessities that are made in practical provisions. There are so many demands now placed upon children and even in this informational age. Many are struggling with understanding the simple things such as gender identification, self-worth, and social acceptance to the point of suicidal contemplation. Part of our fingerprinting privilege in this annoying love mantra is taking time to address small things that to us seem to be a no brainer, but in their young minds they can be very challenging or effacing in nature.

There will never be a limit to the love languages you possess in your spiritual tool belt. That alone can lead them forward every day and help to satisfy the cravings of a heart that hungers for affection from a mom or dad. That is more important than the latest styles of clothing, cell phones, or even housing improvements you can afford to give them while they still sit around your table. Just make sure they are allowed to gather together often with you to reflect the Lord's blessings and see Him reflected in your eyes daily. Imagine the difficulty you will have in telling of God's love for them if you can't even give them your devotion while they reside in your home. Much of what they learn from God they get from you. Your mannerisms. Your language. Your prayer life. Your commitment. And yes, even your daily devotional time. You want to talk about a spiritual ink spot that won't easily go away? Just try measuring yourself daily before them in how you live versus how you want them to learn. The "do what I say and not as I do" mentality used to get great mileage back years ago when life was simpler, but in today's world children aren't buying that bag of goods anymore. They want to see parents who are real in not only how they love but also in how they live. I can remember when I saw our first child, a son and reflected on some prophetic words we had received from Pastor Robert Morris on how in his hour of delivery that the birth would be that of a "supernatural" occurrence. I meditated on that for two weeks and then God gave me a profound message about it (Well almost!). He said simply that it would be a supernatural birth in the hour when it would be needed to bring him into the world. I tried to imagine some kind of extraordinary thing. The reality was his birth only needed some super strength from my wife which God provided at that moment of supreme fatigue, and with a little extra nurse attention, she stepped up the efforts even after twenty hours of hard laboring to bring home the prize. The fingerprint of our love had now been born to us in flesh and blood and our world became better. Yes, even our eyes began to shine brighter because we now understood that God had allowed us to partner with Him for this beautiful creative work. I knew in that moment of holding my little man that God had a purpose for this child and a specific plan for us as parents to help move him forward as a Kingdom person. The calling of God was upon him as it is on every baby that makes it into the world and has its first breath. He was now real in our lives that day, so we had to step up to become real parents for him as well.

The good news for us, now thirty plus years removed is that we are seeing the grandchildren season offer a new but different kind of opportunity and the key we found was in knowing the foundations we were able to provide is now a springboard in their life. Better results can be achieved by purposing the times to stamp the spiritual ink on young hearts so that they too grow up to beget that same foundational capstone in their generation. Our children have to now navigate their path forward with their own children by God's grace and guidance. At least to this place they have chosen to partner in the right spiritual climate. There's a great Hymn of the Church titled *Have Thine On Way Lord* that I have always loved and while I don't often get to hear it played much in the modern church, it still resonates profoundly in my heart. The standout lyric says *thou art the Potter, I am the clay. Mold me and make me after thy will. While I am waiting, yielded and still.* God has often been referred to as the Potter and we His clay, but I would be so bold as to declare that you both, mom and dad are that Potter too! The child that is placed in your hands in the delivery room is the child whom God has placed in your heart for eternity. You're not just their parent for a short season, but you are the life giver of annoying love throughout a lifetime you have been given on this earth. If God so loved the world He gave, then surely you can so love your children and be willing to always give as the demands arise in life.

As new parents would typically count those precious little fingers at birth while they are still but a newborn, you can definitely see the physical fingerprints are already fashioned by God on each hand. No matter how old or how big they get, those refined markings define that child's identity for the rest of their existence and never change. What a remarkable occurrence God does while they are still inside the mother. But what a transcendent privilege we have as parents to shape them with self-identifiable spiritual fingerprints this side of the womb. One is found in tempering the flesh touch of their hands for compassion, while the other is borne by touching a spirit in their hearts with love languages that will make an indelible mark for a lifetime. The latter being the most important because it will help determine how they will choose to position their adult character traits beyond the womb. Ultimately, it will also help position in their heart of hearts where they will spend their life journey in eternity with God beyond the tomb.

Think of it in a child's simple event. As elementary children, many will experience the fun of finger painting either through a social event such as a birthday party, or perhaps even within an art session in their local school. No matter the setting, each child will come away with a masterpiece of artwork painted by those tender hands you first held in your arms while they were barely able to grasp your adult fingers there in the birthing room. Now that precious piece of art in which they used their own hands to creatively make an image with has become a chronicle of love to you as a parent and you endeavor to keep it for as long as you can. Their innocent minds drew freely on this clean paper with only pure love and carefree attention to detail wanting simply to express within their little hands a painting for mom and dad. It's their best effort and their imagination for which they desire to fashion for all to see once they have completed the work. Likewise mom and dad, you have this same opportunity as you pursue your roles in fingerprinting their hearts on the clean canvas of life as well. Sure, you will make splotches of wrong assertions and assessments as you journey forward on your faith canvas but know for certain that your spiritual destiny will be fulfilled with the annoying love attributes you will ink permanently onto their lives. Please understand that just like their artwork or paintings will become more easily recognizable with concise detail as they age, so will your efforts in parenting a faith household with them alongside as well. Your artisan work of family values have a short span of time that covers the opportunity window in which they live under your roof and until they launch out to begin a life of their own. It is during this season of living that your spiritual ink pad needs to be filled with all the necessary ingredients available through God's word and reflected in your heart as a believer who follows Christ. It's in that place of growth where you discover a greater God and a greater grace available for every situation you will encounter. The takeaway will be found in you stepping into your spiritual calling while leaving the mark on their hearts as how you experience God's partnering daily. They will not remember all your personal issues, but they will remember your posture in parenting them through the challenges of being a follower of Christ and how that played out before their eyes. They see, hear, touch, taste and even smell elements of your lifestyle that helps them to retain not only your physical DNA in healthy living but more importantly in spiritual dynamics for growing up. Now that our children are all grown adults, we get reminders from them often of how we did life as their parents from our quirks to our jerks. Some have funny stories of remembrance and only serve for quick laughs, but so many others serve as the fingerprinting elements because we took the time to stamp an ink spot on their heart. However, we believe they received many of the good traits we had to offer them and certainly some not so good ones too. I believe in faith that they received more God traits because we were intentional to pursue those spiritually.

Your faith growth is their Christian example, and they respond accordingly. In the end, you will know success as long as the ink keeps flowing from your hands to your fingers at all times. When you fail to understand that fingerprinting can only happen when the ink stays primed, then you unfortunately lose the ability to stroke the hearts ongoing. There is no reason to run out of resources when you are tethered to God and have all His attributes. He has these available for you to uncover by seeking His ways daily. Think of it in these terms. If your fingertips stay inked up often then every time you touch a life whether it's a family, friend, or foe, you have the chance to leave a significant spiritual mark of yourself. Be sure the ones you leave are ones they will want to carry around as a spiritual tattoo for life. There's nothing worse than a bad tattoo when it goes on display for everyone else to see, so make the fingerprinting count for the best results. Put your holy hands in things that will give you the best spiritual returns as a faith believer exercising that annoying love daily. There is a sweet song lyric that young children often learn in their school or church class that states, *oh be careful little eyes what you see.* It goes on to say *that the Father up above is watching down with love so be careful little eyes what you see*. Mom and dad, the sobering truth is that they are watching you all the time so make sure their eyes see

Father God's heart reflected in your eyes. It's a strategic process to follow through with building faith homes but spiritually inking it to reflect your heart in their lives is well worth the rewards when you see them give it back years later. Your artistic work as parents in creating masterpieces on this life journey allows the final portraits to be inked one spot at a time on their canvas hearts daily by your fingerprints of annoying love.

Chapter Eleven – Measuring the Results

I realize I've given you lot to chew on and think about when it comes to you making your family a household of faith for the Lord. The truth is found in the premise that if it doesn't mean much to you as far as becoming a faith-filled God chaser, then how will you convince your children to catch that same passion. Modeling is making disciples of your family just the same way Jesus did when those twelve rag tag men followed him around for almost three years forsaking their trade and embracing their trials with Jesus. Yes, one failed (Judas) and died because of his wrongful choosing and even another, (Peter) denied Him during a dark time of Jesus's capture by the Romans, but he did recant and come back to the way of following Christ. Think about that! Even with less than a 100% followship of disciples, Jesus, the King of Kings, was still able to turn the world upside down for the gospel mission with those who remained faithful to His command to follow Him. I understand that we all would love for our children to end up being or doing life in a certain way when it comes to their Christian faith, but the reality is they have to live their moments within the constraints of their heart or calling. Sometimes that means they take a different path that may or may not ever find its way back to the cross of Christ for reconciliation in receiving their salvation within our lifetime. However, as parents we still have to cling to the hope of God's word that before they end their life's journey, they too will have gained the necessary influences from the home life we provided as a witness of the Christian faith to choose God's forgiveness. We can't always know how the hearts and minds of people think or how they respond when difficulties and life challenges begin to close in on them, but the important thing is that God always sees and knows their path.

I'm reminded of a lady who was in her last moments of life having received a stage four cancer diagnosis in previous weeks, but only had a few days left to be on this earth. We had known her for many years crossing paths often at birthday gatherings as her daughter had been a neighbor and close friend of ours. She had asked if I would come pray with her at her home before she became unresponsive to any more communication. At that time, I was on staff as one of our church pastors, so my wife and I were honored to be able to go and share Christ with her before she passed. While this woman never paid much homage to a "having a Christian faith or local church attendance" for most of her life, here at death's door she found the revelation and grace from God to receive this glorious gift of salvation just before her life would expire. The real tragedy was that she would never know what a legacy of what her faith could have done for her during her most productive times of living her life on earth. Thankfully, her only adopted daughter did have that relationship experience with Christ which she modeled before her mom and helped plant seeds along the way. The ultimate triumph was that she died with peace and assurance that Jesus Christ had provided her forgiveness and carried her home to the reward of eternal life in Heaven. Needless to say, the funeral was made much more comforting in knowing where she would spend her everlasting home away from this earth. I've been fortunate to have had this kind of death's door opportunity to be at someone's bedside on multiple occasions and to be there to offer hope for those fast approaching a final breath. While the woman I mentioned above was able to choose to pray the prayer of salvation as she could still speak and be coherent, the other gentleman who was a long-time neighbor did not have the consciousness to be vocally expressive. I have held to the belief that through my simple words at his bedside that he was able to think those word thoughts in his heart to pray to receive Christ. I will only ever know for certain when I get to Heaven myself if that was his final destination. You never know when your time will expire here on planet earth and in many cases while it may not have been your "time to go," some freak accident, or event could have shortened your life in an instant. I'm sure some reading this statement maybe thinking, *that's not true because God knows all, and He knows the very moment when you will die.* Yes, I agree wholeheartedly but God allows us the opportunity to choose life or death daily in the scope of our living, but some such as those who choose to end their own life prematurely may have cut short their future expiration time as a result of a choice.

Without digressing and spending more time on opening this "can of worms" perspective, I will suffice it to say that we have an important job as faith people both from a parent and believer's perspective. We should strive to understand that our time is very precious, and thus we must redeem the opportunities we have to impact other's lives. The two stories I shared above depicted a familiar situation for many today as I observed that there wasn't much of a Christian faith-based life built in the home by either of the elderly people mentioned unfortunately. In the latter case since there was no legacy opportunity left with any children to be passed on to, it created a sad revelation for the surviving spouse that she had no one to share her sunset season of life with now being childless. Fortunately, she was able to move back to her hometown and be close to her brother and spend her final days with family. My hope is that she remembered the words we shared with her husband to receive Christ and perhaps made a choice for herself later on as well. For those of us who are still sharing lives with others daily, the takeaway is found in realizing we have such a short window of opportunity that seems to close faster each year with so much assault and challenge coming from every direction against our families. We must put on our faith fashioned combat boots and wade through the muck and mire of life in order to get the ultimate spiritual results we desire. So what do those results look like you ask? Let me begin to provide the answer by offering some food for thought. If you never inspect what you expect then all you have to measure your life with is unrealistic outcomes based on nothing more than conjecture and reasoning. One of the main reasons sports have an appeal to fan cultures is because everyone likes keeping score to conclude who wins and who loses. Not only do people choose sides, make bets, and gather in droves to celebrate their team with tailgating, many really get way over into almost craziness just to demonstrate their commitment. I appreciate fandom as much as the next guy but honestly there's no need to be too far out there when the final results are only reflective of a game and not life itself. If we could only channel some of that energy for Kingdom Building, then we would certainly advance the gospel beyond where it is now and keep growing the faith at a stronger pace. Imagine how that would look like on Sundays!

Be that as it may, there is a reasonable saneness to want to win at all costs no matter what. As parents, this should echo emphatically within your heart as it relates to your children and your home. No rational person intentionally marries their spouse, decides to have kids, and then prays for failure while they are going through this life journey. As crazy as it sounds, not setting the right measurements could create that effect unfortunately. Goals are good and can be very helpful to keep focus on priorities for where you want to go in life, but more importantly they should be tools to live by as you are moving your family forward in faith. Just as you would have your cars serviced, home inspected for pests, or even get medical and dental check-ups, these necessary services help you keep the condition of your assets in good working order. In like manner, why not evaluate your relationships with family and friends to determine if you are making the right spiritual choices to support your Christian values. Some of these persons may be the supportive and challenging types to help you keep sharpening the spiritual irons of cutting-edge decision making while others may be dragging you down a wrong path. Only you can choose who needs to have more of your time and who should not. Same thing goes for almost every area of your life, including you or your spouse all the way down to your family's lifestyle. Obviously, building a strong marriage requires effort and work to find the right foundations for your home but as you do it models itself to those who are in your inner circle. Everything from the television you watch daily, to your habits of food choices, and even to your hygiene can play a role in shaping your faith as you are on display around the clock in your home. The Bible teaches us to be excellent in what is good and innocent of evil. When that really does happen it sets the stage for the God of peace to effectively crush Satan underneath the faith of those believers. Life is without a doubt a marathon, but parenting is only a short journey in that life running. It doesn't require a lifetime of household management on our part, yet it does employ a small window of opportunity that has to be addressed in its timeframe of demand. The key to your results and the measurement of your successes will be found outside that viewing window. It's then that you can begin to see your adult children as having been launched out of the nest, while assuming the same heart for God just as you faithfully instilled into them. We've all seen the nature portrayals of an eaglet being cared for and finally reaching its full growth journey, only to be celebrated by its mother removing its nesting feeding rights. The now fully matured eagle offspring suddenly has lost his home. But in an instant of inborn instinct it now embraces the wings given inherently to make a life change in soaring far beyond its tree top boundaries. Success has a triumph and while your offspring may seem unsteady or uncertain in their initial launch into adult life you can rest with assurance. Because you have waited before the Lord with an annoying love for your children, they too will have the renewed strength to mount up with their faith developed wings and fly as well. Their independent soaring is your scoring a win for the Kingdom of Heaven and an internal satisfaction. You now have a knowing that no matter what happens, they have the necessary ingredients inside of them to handle what life may bring their way. Very often it takes a longer time than we anticipate. However, the best cream always rises to the top and it becomes the sweetest taste of victory in that God has allowed you to have played a specific role in their lives. Well done good and faithful parents! Enjoy your adults and get ready for the second helping of freestyle parenting with your grandchildren. They are absolutely a reward and a heritage from your children. The really good thing is you get all the choice benefits without having to do most of the work the second time around.

As we close this chapter, I want to leave you with some final thoughts. What may seem as an annoying love to your family during your home life season with your children is really the very thing they will remember as it defines your heart. It can often redefine their minds as well. They won't always remember those small things that challenged and annoyed them about your parenting as time goes by but be assured that they will reflect often on your examples of love and sacrifice. There were key moments which helped to shape their lives into becoming men and women of God. The measure of your parenting efforts as a leader will be found in them now becoming involved as you were to them. Like you in some ways but only better in having received the spiritual baton from living in your home as a kid while learning firsthand how to become a child of the most-high God. When a family's faith can duplicate itself forward into future generations it creates a wealth of spiritual growth. From that point you have reached the pinnacle of what your stewardship as a parent has been all about. That is the ultimate goal of your spiritual focus for how to parent. In Christ we live, move, and have our being on this earth as believers in God. Doors are now open for choosing to follow this clear path of faith by grace.

Time always proves the pudding in the mix, and that which you develop in one life will yield a legacy of harvest in the life blessings that come as a result. Truthfully, we will never fully understand or be able to measure the cause and effect of what our annoying love mantra will do for our children as well as other family and friends. It's safe to conclude that while the half may never be told this side of Heaven regarding the impacts and of how we served our children in parenting, there is a reward awaiting our commitment of faithfulness. God has never called anyone to a measure of output quota per se, but He has and does continue to expect those who receive His grace of salvation to be obedient to this privilege. This is required and will be measured at the pearly gate arrival in order for us to enter into that ultimate reward. It is only what we do with Jesus that matters at our journey's end. If we have embraced His finished work, then we can and will join Heaven's redeemed multitude. Hopefully, you have, or will, accept Him as your Savior and by doing so keep pointing your children and others to this saving grace of faith. Hopefully, they too will continue in that journey to the end as you have provided the right example in your life. The Bible teaches that life is fleeting, and we are but a vapor which appears for a short while and then is gone. While we may reach seventy, eighty or even more years of living on this planet, when our time expires it won't be what we leave behind that matters but rather what we send ahead. Your family and friends may only have you as their Bible to read and may only be able to measure God's grace by watching your faith play out before them. If that is the case, then surely you understand what your responsibility can create in a household of faith. This is not to put a heavy on you and create a burden of stress, but instead it is a yoke of ease to generate a mindset of blessing to move others toward their spiritual journey in finding God and *Building Family Faith*. You have what it takes in Jesus to finish the job so go and do it well!

Appendix- 5 Steps for Help

I hope you've gotten some inspiration in reading this book regarding the Spirit of an *Annoying Love: Building Family Faith,* but I wanted to leave you with some thoughts and practical takeaways for how to get stated or even how to make steps for pursuing this love mantra.

Step 1

First and foremost, for this kind of love to work you should have a personal relationship with Jesus Christ as your Lord and Savior. If you haven't made that decision yet or taken that plunge just simply pray this prayer. Whoever calls on the name of the Lord will be saved by His grace!

> *Lord Jesus, I realize that I'm a sinner and have missed the mark in living my life away from your great love for me. I ask you today to come into my heart and life and bring your forgiveness and grace to give me a new heart to follow after you. I receive your love for me now and ask you to come in my heart to be by Lord and Savior. In your Holy son's name I pray. Thank you for saving me Lord Jesus. Amen.*

If you prayed this prayer, please let someone know immediately (we'd love to hear about it too!) and contact your local church, a friend or Pastor to follow through with confirming your salvation. Prepare with your church leaders to get your water baptism so you can substantiate your faith foundations going forward as to not create doubts in your salvation future.

Step 2

Begin developing a devotional time for yourself so that you build your spirit man stronger and start getting the word of God activated in your heart and life. It's not about the volume of Bible books you read but more importantly how you understand scriptures, so that element can help transform your mind to be less carnal and more spiritual. There are lots of good devotional books to help you in this journey. I recommend one titled, *Jesus Calling,* by Sarah Young which has something for every day of the year. Also take time to journal with note taking as well and use that as an informational and questioning opportunity to ask the Holy Spirit to teach you during your devotional time. Similarly, take time to do another devotion your children at bedtime or some other time and allow them to participate in reading, praying, and practicing the scriptures. I used my children's bedtime time to read, pray and act out many Bible stories as character play time. Their favorite was always David and Goliath because they got to smite (more like a toy sword whack) dad down with a sling and sword and declare their victory. It's amazing what they will remember about the Bible over time and how that fingerprinting piece will begin to ink their hearts for life. My children still laugh about those moments even today so be creative with them.

Step 3

Find a Bible based church that allows the expression of the Holy Spirit to be involved in its ministry and get activated in it through serving, giving, and attending. Part of your significant growth in learning about God will be greatly enhanced by being faithful in bringing your family to the House of God and seeing Him build their hearts in faith foundations. Psalms tells that those who are planted in the house of God will flourish in the gates of His presence so make this a vital piece of your spiritual life and development. Our children spent many years and hours being involved in all facets of the church life such as choirs, classes, homeschool co-ops, Kids Camps, music, and drama. Plus, we utilized many other avenues of activity that helped shape their life with unique talents that helped advance them for future life endeavors as well. The Church arena is a critical part of that village community and is important for developing their social and spiritual environment so make sure you choose well and integrate fully where your family can thrive. Mom and dad should reflect this lifestyle too and lead them by examples.

Step 4

Continue to be faithful in Steps 1 to 3 so that as a leader or parent you grow yourself into the person of faith God desires for you to become. There are no shortcuts to the faith life, but you can accelerate this lifestyle by staying committed and being faithful along your journey ongoing. Beyond these Steps just begin to take measures that are intentional and consistent in all avenues of your family's life. Everything from birthdays to holidays to special days need to be celebrated whether big or small in outcome so that you promote those important things that create memories of your home to be modeled later on by your children. Always take time for the small things when they matter to your family as these will mushroom into bigger issues if they aren't giving attention and support. The toughest part of your journey as a parent and leader is staying faithful in the small and mundane things because they aren't as exciting as the bigger events, but they can offer more advantages because they provide the leverage needed for consistency and commitment.

Step 5

Rinse and Repeat! Yeah, in relevant clothes washing terms obviously. No doubt you fully understand how the laundry never seems to end so use this mindset as you go along knowing that there is always a light at the end of the tunnel, but there's still a tunnel. Write down your family's vision and communicate it with everyone often. Always refer back to it and modify as needed for requirements and maybe some necessary accommodations. Never apologize for how you intend to do spiritual faith in your family. Some things with your children take time to sink in so keep enforcing and supporting without getting exasperated. Let them be a part of household chores as well as choosing fun family things together. Take time to get away and make memories often with family, friends, and in fellowship events. Make sure discipline and discipleship are two sides of the same coin. Teach them to give as they live, serve as they are being served, and love others without measure. What you model before them they will repeat in their life whether good or bad so be aware of bad mouths and habits.

Finally, have fun and enjoy the journey. You don't get a second chance for a first impression, but you do get new days each morning to do something impactful and long lasting that they will remember beyond the home life. Your marriage and your money tell the story of what you value the most in your life so make sure you steward this according to the word of God and that your decisions to live a certain way of life helps to promote what you are Building Family Faith for. My wife and I are proof that flawed people can still get maximum benefits from a simple but faithful trust in God who adds His grace often and on time. Be assured He will do the same for you and your family as long as you stay on the right path of following Jesus Christ daily!

About the Author

James (Jamie) Pettit has been involved in Christian Ministry for over thirty-five years. He has served in ministry as Executive Pastor, Lead Pastor, and as a Worship Leader among other Church Leadership roles. He has a passion in serving others by expressively encouraging and equipping believers through his spiritual gifts used in singing, preaching, teaching, writing, and webcasting within online social media platforms. Jamie's music ministry endeavors have included recording a Contemporary Christian album (*My Praise To You*) as well as other song singles as a gospel artist. For over thirty years, Jamie has participated in Worship in Conferences and Concerts as a lead vocalist and singer/songwriter. As a staff Pastor he's written many church manuals, ministry publications, teaching, equipping lay ministers and also featured as a Conference speaker.

Additionally, Jamie has shared his heart and talents on TV, Radio, Community Events, Social Media platforms, and through numerous local churches as well as missionary travels around the world with Global Ministry Teams. He is founder of *The Church Revolution*, an online para-church ministry support webcast shared on his YouTube channel, Twitter, Facebook, and Instagram. Jamie currently serves his local church as part of their Prayer Counsel Ministry Team as well as a front-line vocalist for the Worship Team at Hope Church - Spartanburg, SC.

Jamie has worked fulltime and part-time for multiple churches where he served in Pastoral and Lay ministry roles. Professionally, he has spent the majority of his full-time business career within his financial acumen in various Accounting and Management leadership roles. He received his BA degree in Accounting from

Wofford College, and MBA Graduate degree from Grand Canyon University. If you would like to connect with Jamie Pettit for future ministry engagements, you can email your requests to Jamie Pettit at sing4prayz@charter.net.

Also feel free to follow us on Twitter *@jprevolution*, Instagram – jamie.pettit.007, YouTube Channel @ https://youtube.com/channel/UCE51GX2SlByvUVrgci-VVVw, or our ministry page at Facebook - *The Church Revolution*.